The Trail Guide to the Microsoft® Network

A rapid-reading reference to using and cruising the Microsoft Network online service

MELODY NEWROCK

Addison-Wesley Publishing Company
Reading, Massachusetts • Menlo Park, California
New York • Don Mills, Ontario • Wokingham, England
Amsterdam • Bonn • Sydney • Singapore • Tokyo
Madrid • San Juan • Paris • Seoul • Milan
Mexico City • Taipei

Library of Congress Cataloging-in-Publication Data

Newrock, Melody.

The trail guide to the Microsoft network: a rapid-reading reference to using and cruising the Microsoft Network online service / Melody Newrock.

p. cm.

Includes index.

ISBN 0-201-48943-0

1. Microsoft Network (Online service) I. Title

QA76.57.M52N49 1996

025.04--dc20 95-45146

CIP

Sponsoring Editor: Kim Fryer
Project Manager: Sarah Weaver
Production Coordinator: Erin Sweeney
Cover design: Barbara Atkinson
Set in 11 point Palatino by ST Associates

1 2 3 4 5 6 7 8 9 -DOH- 0099989796
First printing, December 1995

Addison-Wesley books are available for bulk purchases by corporations, institutions, and other organizations. For more information please contact the Corporate, Government, and Special Sales Department at (800) 238-9682.

Find us on the World-Wide Web at:
http://www.aw.com/devpress/

Dedication

To the very special small people in my life, Travis and Juliette, whose cooperation made this book possible, and whose existence made it necessary!

And for Steve; his continued faith in a successful outcome kept me going through some very long nights.

Contents

Acknowledgments

Particular thanks go to Kim Fryer, my patient editor at Addison-Wesley. Throughout the long MSN beta period, her unswerving belief that this book would indeed one day be finished was a constant source of amazement and encouragement. Additional thanks go to Sarah Weaver and Erin Sweeney for their exceptionally rapid turnaround of the manuscript once it was finished—a writer's dream is forever to write, and a production process that takes no time at all. We came very close to this at both ends!

Forgiveness, rather than thanks, is probably due my husband, Steve Guty, who suggested this project to me in the first place.

I'd like to also thank all the Microsoft people and other MSN beta testers who were of enormous help in keeping me apprised of ever-changing schedules, content providers, and user interfaces, along with a steady supply of tips and tricks. And a special thanks is due to Janet Reno and her staff at the Department of Justice for their cameo role, in not blocking MSN by injunction.

Introduction

From its inception, the Microsoft Network (MSN) was designed to change the way we think and feel about commercial on-line services. In its final beta test, it already had over 10,000 subscribers and scores of independent content providers, or ICPs. The content providers ranged from huge corporations to small businesses, looking to make the information highway work for them!

As a Windows 95 user you will feel comfortable from the first moment you sign on to the Microsoft Network. If you know how to use Windows 95, you already know how to navigate the Microsoft Network. If you don't know how to use Windows 95 yet, this book will serve as a complete guide through the Network. It will quickly make the very logical MSN interface second nature. Opening and closing windows, dragging and dropping icons, and single- and double-clicking for item selection will all be familiar.

The World at Your Fingertips

Imagine having the ability (to say nothing of the time) to meet with thousands of people from all over the world, all sharing your interests. With a click of the mouse, enter a chat "room." Type in a sentence or two and start a conversation. It's a great way to make new friends. You never have to worry about how you're dressed or how you look.

Communications

Look in on a bulletin board devoted to rock climbing in the Andes or to model trains. Have a question about the latest ski equipment? Post it on a bulletin board and wait for a reply. Advice will be on the way. You can read messages, follow conversations, and download files.

Attend live chat sessions where you can talk to and ask questions of people you would otherwise never have an opportunity to contact, including politicians, businesspeople and rock stars. Or arrange to meet someone for a private chat on-line.

Once you get to know others in the on-line community, use the extensive E-Mail services. You can download your messages and read them at your leisure off-line, or you can read them on-line and immediately shoot off a reply. E-Mail others on the Microsoft Network, send mail to people on other on-line services such as CompuServe and America Online or take advantage of the seamless interface to the Internet.

The Information Highway—Access to the Internet

We've all heard about the information highway, and that road is now well paved. The Microsoft Network allows full access to the Internet—a worldwide computer network. You'll be able to send and receive electronic mail through the Internet and have full access to newsgroups. Imagine striking up a conversation with someone in

England or Japan as easily as sending a memo to a colleague in the next office.

Information Resources

You can browse through Encarta, an on-line encyclopedia. Or spend some time with the Microsoft Bookshelf, a collection of reference tools including a dictionary, thesaurus, atlas, and more. With the click of your mouse, find all the information in the dictionary on a given word or look up the same word in all the publications at once.

Check in a few times a day to follow the news, get a weather report, or find out how the Yankees did last night. Keeping track of your stock portfolio has never been so easy, with quotes and company information instantly available.

But the Microsoft Network is much more than a way of accessing information. It is a truly interactive service. The Microsoft Network allows you to *do* things more easily and conveniently than any other on-line service.

Shopping On-line

Do you hate the hassle of shopping in a crowded mall or department store? Shopping on-line allows you to order anything you can find in a store—from anthologies to zoom lenses—without getting up from your desk. You can often get brand-name products from respected manufacturers at better prices, delivered right to your door.

The Microsoft Network Difference

By now you may be thinking, "OK, but a lot of this sounds like the stuff offered on other on-line services, what's so special about this one?"

Well, aside from the fact that Microsoft has made it easy to get around in MSN, there's a *lot* that's special about this service. Let's start with the content itself. Because MSN gives so much flexibility to providers of services, there will be many more of them, offering many different service options. And because the minimum connect time per month is low, it costs little to get started. Additional charges are based on time plans you may or may not select, along with any additional services you choose. So *you* are in control of your costs, which can really be quite minimal!

Other on-line services have bulletin boards, or areas for public discussion, but not like MSN's. There's the way the bulletin boards actually perform. Members have the ability to view an entire "map," or outline, of a conversation without having to read all postings and replies. And those postings and replies can be fully formatted, with various fonts, colors, sizes, and so on. You can create "shortcuts" to include in your messages that will perform a specified task. For example, they can download a file to and open a word processor, download a file to be accessed later, or just send the reader to another area on the Microsoft Network.

Using simple "drag and drop" technology, copying files to your computer has never been easier. No more hassles with obscure paths, file names, or protocols (now, was that X-Modem or Z-Modem? Or Kermit!?).

The Electronic Mail on MSN is fully integrated with Microsoft Exchange, which can be fully integrated with all your on-line messaging, off-line composing, and electronic faxing as well. Just as with bulletin boards, "shortcuts" and attachments can be included in your E-Mail.

Do you ever wish you had the time to attend courses on using Microsoft products? Courses on software never seem to be made available at a convenient time or location. Log on to MSN and enroll in the Microsoft On-line Institute. Here you will find low-cost electronic self-study courses and courseware. In addition, you can enter virtual classrooms, complete with instructors and other students. Using E-Mail and bulletin boards, an instructor will provide course assignments, set progress goals, and answer questions. All from the convenience of your desktop!

Perhaps you want to start your own forum. Or, have you ever thought there must be some way to make money with your computer? Start a new business, or grow your current one on-line. Microsoft will provide the tools and information you need to get started.

Read on, and learn how to take advantage of this fabulous tool. The world awaits you!

CHAPTER 1

Getting Started

Now that you understand how exciting this revolutionary new on-line service is, you're probably anxious to get started. This chapter explains in detail what you need to know and what software and hardware you will need to have installed on your computer system to do just that.

As of this writing you must have an IBM PC or 100 percent compatible computer running the Microsoft Windows 95 or later operating system. If you are unsure which version of Windows you have, refer to Figures 1.1 and 1.2 and compare them to what you see on your computer monitor. If you just upgraded to Windows 95, or if you have a new computer where Windows 95 had been factory-installed, one of these was probably the first screen you saw upon booting up your system. You may have a different number of icons, or they may appear slightly different, from those shown here.

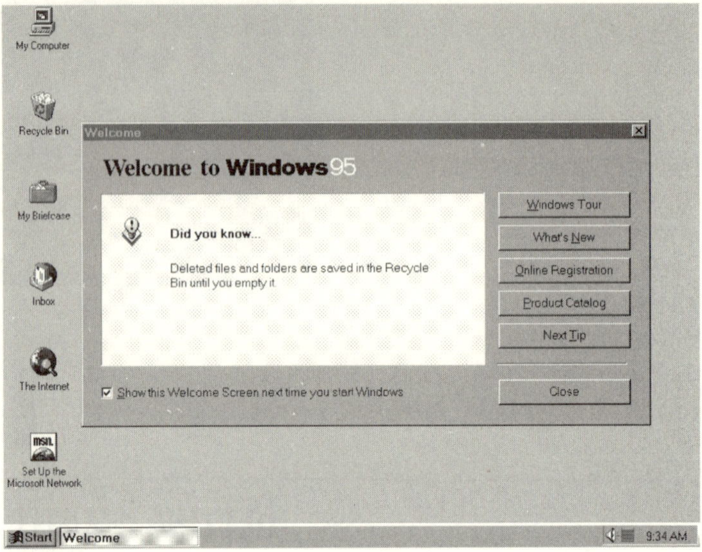

Figure 1.1 *After installation of Windows 95, this is the first window you see. By checking the box in the lower left, it will return each time you start up Windows 95.*

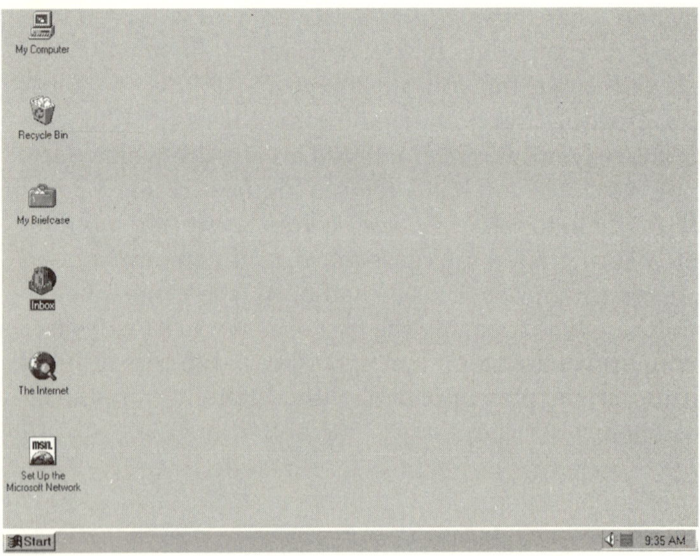

Figure 1.2 *The Windows 95 Desktop without the Welcome window.*

If you have already been running Windows 95 and have checked the "Do not display this opening screen" box in Figure 1.1, then Figure 1.2 will appear as your basic desktop. If your screen resembles the one in Figure 1.3, you have Windows 3.x, and Windows 95 must be installed on your computer in order to access the Microsoft Network.

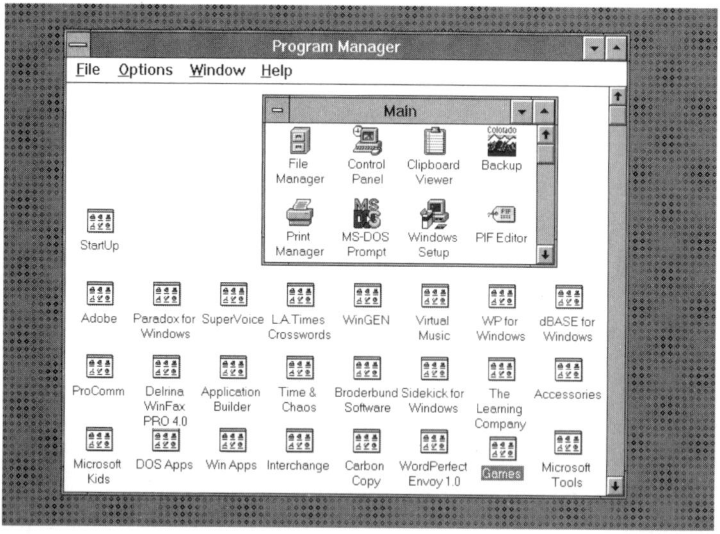

Figure 1.3 *A Windows 3.1 Desktop. If this is what appears on your monitor, you will have to upgrade to Windows 95 to access the Microsoft Network.*

You must also have a modem—the device that connects the computer to a basic telephone line and enables it to send data in digital form back and forth to the Microsoft Network. It may also be used to send faxes or log on to other on-line services. It may be an external modem, which sits along side the computer, or an internal one, which works invisibly, but not noiselessly, from inside the computer.

If you will be purchasing a modem, pay particular attention to the modem speed, usually referred to as the baud rate, or bits per second (BPS). Slow modems are 2,400 baud (BPS); faster ones are 9,600–28,800 baud. By early 1996 MSN may support even faster modems—up to 115,000 baud—using ISDN (integrated services digital network) technology. Although the faster modems are generally more expensive, you will be on-line for shorter periods of time, and downloading files will be much faster and, therefore, less expensive.

Setting Up Your Modem

If you are adding a modem for the first time *after* installing Windows 95, you must let Windows know that there is a new device to be configured for your system. This will in some ways be very similar to installing the Microsoft Network software and will certainly be just as easy!

Using the Windows 95 Control Panel

1. Install your modem according to the manufacturer's directions.
2. Click the Start button on the left side of the task bar. Select Settings and then Control Panel (Figure 1.4).
3. Double-click the Add New Hardware icon.
4. The first screen to appear merely states what the Add New Hardware Wizard does. The next screen to appear, Install New Modem, gives the option of having Windows *not* automatically detect your modem. For now, do not check this item, and let Windows 95 do the work for you. Click the Next button.
5. When the third Add New Hardware Wizard appears, click the Next button.
6. Make sure all other programs are shut down. This may take several minutes. You can see that progress is being made by the movement of the VBX control at the bottom of the dialog box (Figure 1.5). If it seems to get stuck towards the end, take heart and give it some

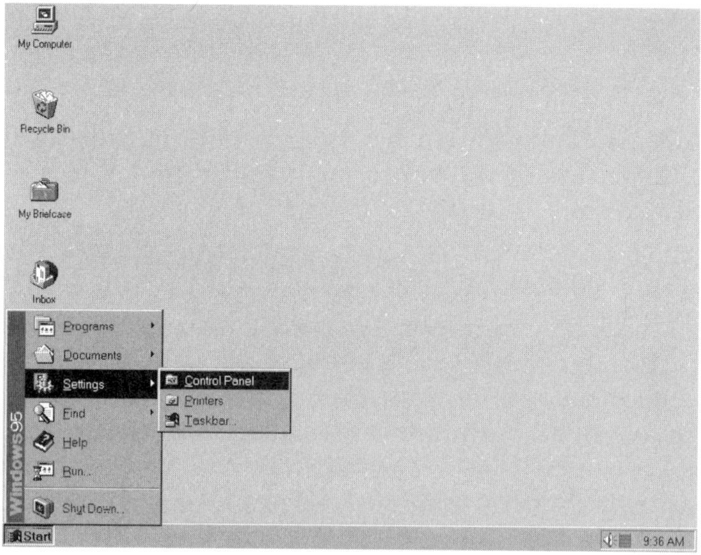

Figure 1.4 *The Start button is where to go to launch programs other than those on the Desktop. From here the Control Panel enables you to add or remove hardware or software.*

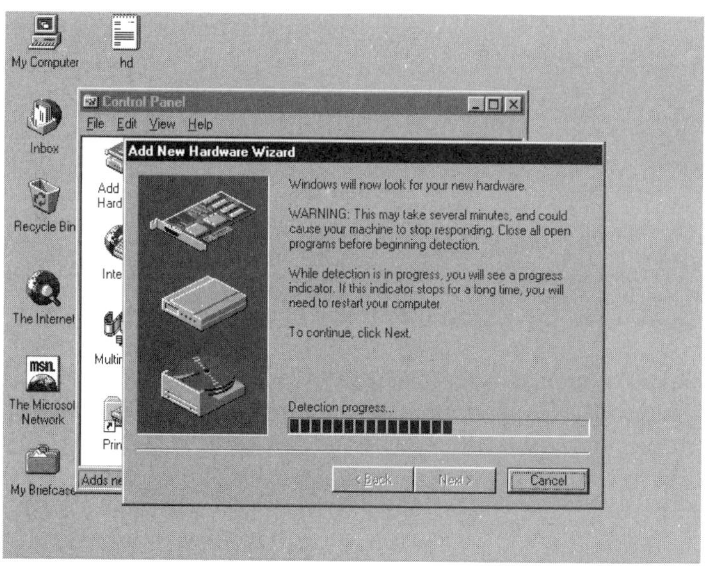

Figure 1.5 *Windows will try to automatically detect any new hardware, including modems, that you install.*

more time, and then perhaps some more time! Listen to the cranking sounds coming from the hard disk drive. You should be hearing irregular sounds, indicating that something is indeed going on.

7. When successful, Windows will inform you that it has finished detecting your hardware. Click Finish.
8. Check to see if the serial port and modem type are correct (Figure 1.6). Click Next to continue. If the information is incorrect, click Change and continue from step 1 below under Manual Installation.

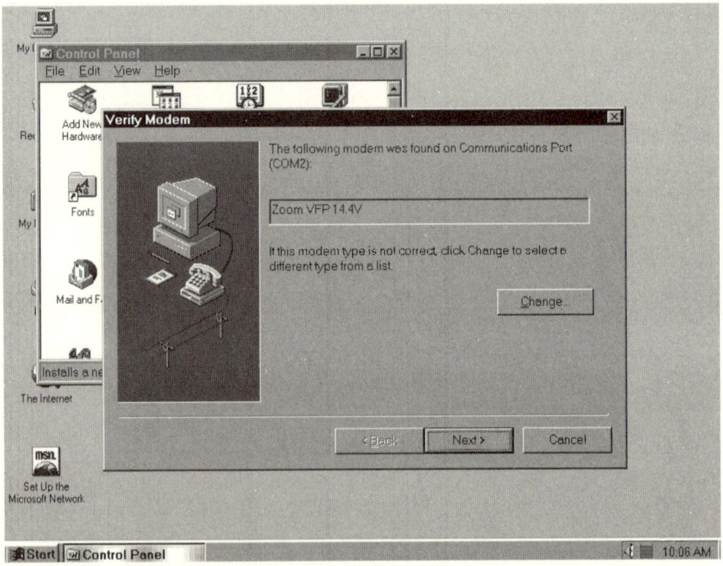

Figure 1.6 *If successful at detecting your configuration, Windows 95 will inform you of what it found, and any necessary device drivers will be added to your configuration.*

9. When you return to the Modems Properties box, you will notice your modem as a listed device. Click on Dialing Properties.

   The Dialing Properties (Figure 1.7) box is where you provide the general characteristics of your phone line and where you may change your default location. Here you can store properties and phone numbers for different locations, a useful feature if you travel with your computer.

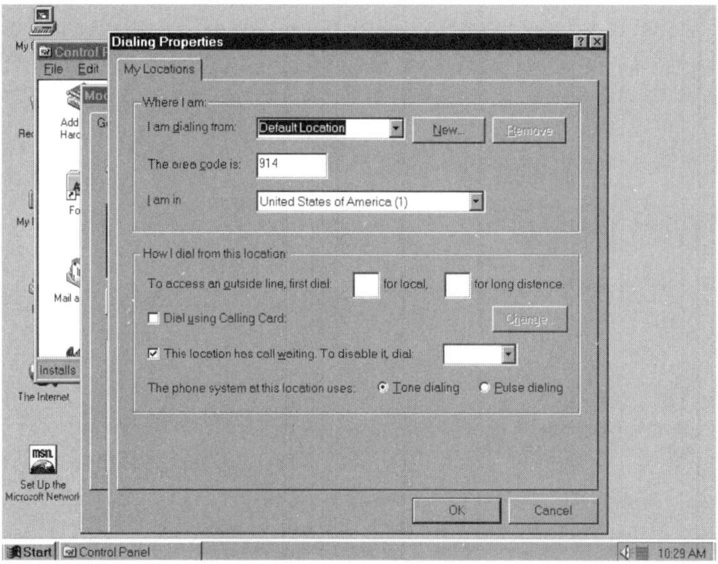

Figure 1.7 *The Dialing Properties box strives to give you whatever's needed to finish the communications installation yourself, no matter how complex the phone system or situation.*

Here you also tell MSN how to get an outside line, whether to use a telephone credit card, and the credit card number.

Tone or pulse dialing must be specified. Tone is usually known as touch-tone dialing, and pulse uses a standard rotary dial phone. Be aware that some push button phones are really using the pulse dialing mechanism, and just look like touch-tone phones.

If you have Call Waiting, it must be disabled. Otherwise, every time an incoming call comes in, you will be disconnected! If you do not know what the code is to disable it (it's generally *66), call your local phone company. Last, if there is no local access number in your area, check the Dial as a long distance call box.

10. Click OK to return to Modems Properties and Close to back out (or you will go through the entire process again!)

    Close the Control Panel window, and your modem is successfully installed.

Manual Installation

1. If Windows cannot identify your modem type, you are presented with the list in Figure 1.8.

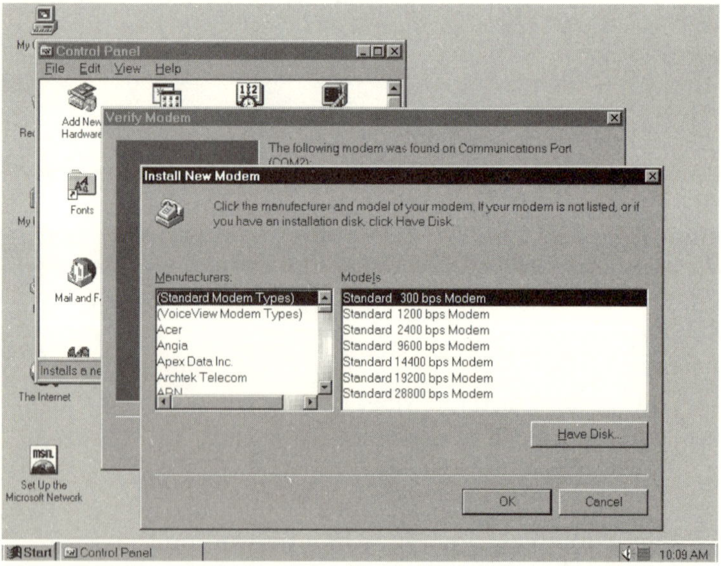

Figure 1.8 *If Windows 95 cannot detect your modem, you are presented with a vast array of makes and models from which to choose.*

2. The left side of this dialog box presents a list of modem manufacturers. Using the mouse, scroll down until you see your modem listed and highlight your selection.
3. The right side is a list of specific models. Again, scroll down until you are able to highlight the correct model.
4. Click the Next button to go on.
5. You must now tell Windows which port your modem is using. Figure 1.9 shows a typical list of available ports and any devices Windows detects. Select the correct item, then click the Finish button. If your modem is not listed, select "Standard Modem." Your modem will make optimal high-speed connections using its default factory settings. You will not be able, however, to change some of its settings, such as its speaker volume.

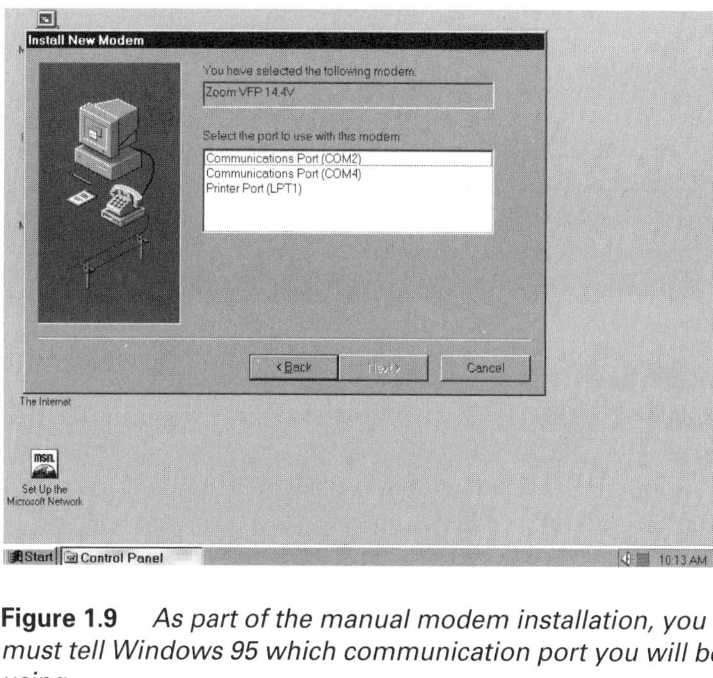

Figure 1.9 *As part of the manual modem installation, you must tell Windows 95 which communication port you will be using.*

The Microsoft Network supports error correction and data compression as long as your modem does. However, these features are not supported if you are forced to install your modem as the "Standard Modem."

6. If the device listing dialog box reappears, click Cancel.
7. Upon return of the Install Modems box, click Dialing Properties. Continue from step 11 in the preceding installation instructions.

Installing the Microsoft Network Software

You should have already established whether or not you are currently running Windows 95. If you will be installing Windows 95 for the first time, and if you are not an advanced user, choose the Typical installation (or Portable, if that's what you are using) under Setup Options. The Windows 95 Setup Wizard, several dialog boxes down the road, will present you with a box titled Communicate with Anyone. Just make sure that you select The Microsoft Network, even if you do not need the other two options, Microsoft Mail and Microsoft Fax.

Installing the software after Windows 95 is already installed is also accomplished quite easily.

Installation from the Control Panel

If the Set Up the Microsoft Network icon (see Figure 1.2, just above the Start button) does not appear on your monitor, you will need to install the software from the Control Panel. Don't panic! Microsoft has made this very easy.

The Add/Remove Programs Properties dialog box can be accessed from Settings/Control Panel on the task bar. The Control Panel is where you change and adjust many different components in your system, such as adding or removing software, changing the date and time, or adjusting the way the mouse behaves.

1. Click the Start button on the left side of the task bar, point to Settings, and then click Control Panel.
2. Select Add/Remove Programs, which should be in the top row.
3. Notice the tabs at the top of the Add/Remove Programs Properties screen (Figure 1.10). Click the Windows Setup tab to see the list of Windows components.

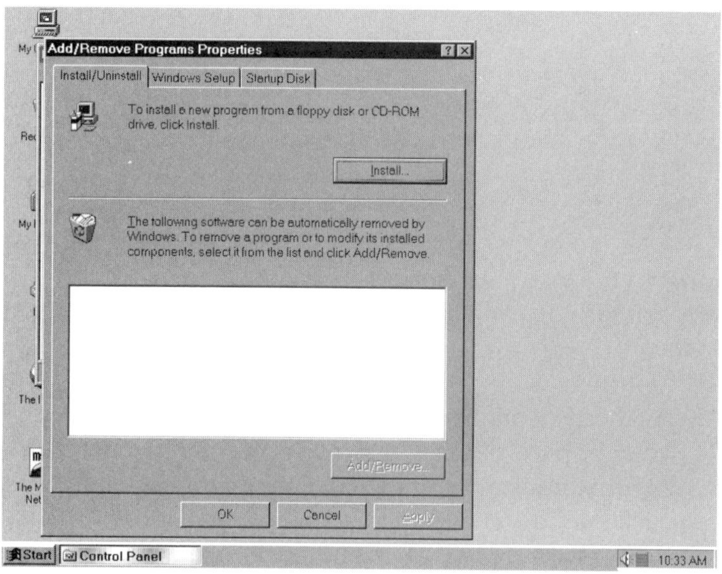

Figure 1.10 *If there is no Setup the Microsoft Network icon on the desktop, use Add/Remove Programs from the Control Panel.*

4. Using the scroll bar on the right hand side of the window, move down until you can select The Microsoft Network. In most cases, you'll also get a message telling you that Microsoft Exchange will have to be installed as well—that's fine, because it's needed (Figure 1.11). Click Yes and then OK to continue.

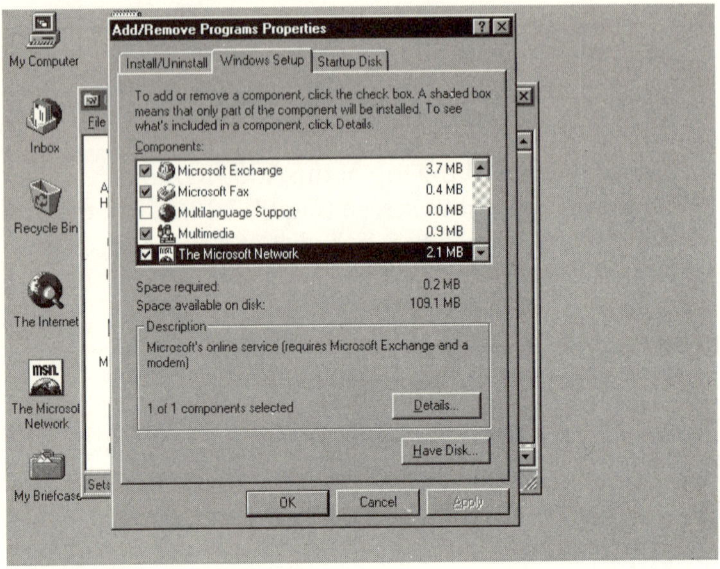

Figure 1.11 *Windows Setup serves a wide range of software options you can add after Windows 95 has already been installed.*

5. As the system files are copied, a dialog box will keep you apprised of what is being copied and the percentage that has been completed. At any time you may click the Cancel button to stop the installation. After all the files are copied, Microsoft Exchange will be configured and set up. Exchange is where you will review, receive, compose, and send your electronic mail.
6. The Inbox Wizard (your mail is delivered to Inbox) asks if you have ever used Microsoft Exchange. Click the No radio button and then Next to continue.
7. Windows will need to know which information service you want to use with Microsoft Exchange for electronic mail. Select the Microsoft Network On-line Service and then Next to continue.

8. Click Next again and then let the Setup Wizard know whether you want to have the Inbox in the StartUp group. Including it means that it will automatically run every time you start Windows. Click the Next button to move on.
9. Done! Click Finish to have Windows create Shortcuts to be placed on the Desktop, allowing you easy access to the Microsoft Network and to your Electronic Mail Inbox.
10. Close the Control Panel window.

The Microsoft Network makes frequent use of a word processor or other editor. If you do not have a word processor, open the Windows Setup box and make sure that the Accessories box has been checked and that Wordpad has been installed. Rather than take up valuable connect time, MSN will very often download files to your computer using Wordpad, a mini word-processor. You can then read or print the files immediately or save to disk and work with them off-line.

Preparing for Registration

1. Double-click the Microsoft Network icon, which is now on your desktop.
2. The next window gives you a brief introduction to the Microsoft Network and verifies that you are not already an MSN member (Figure 1.12). Click OK to continue.
3. Fill in your country's location, your area code, any number you need to access an outside line (if necessary), and your touch-tone or pulse (rotary) dialing status. Click OK to continue.

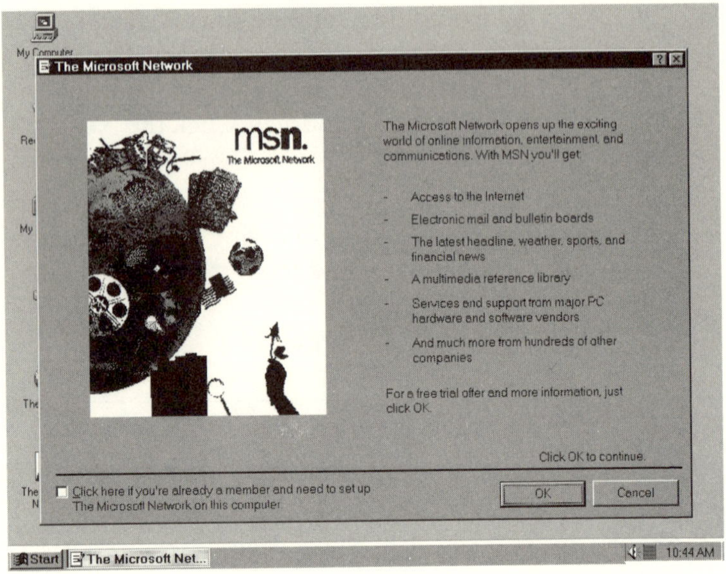

Figure 1.12 *If a Microsoft Network account has previously been set up, you can specify that this is a new installation but not a new account.*

4. Fill in the next window. Your area code should already be filled in; add to it your local exchange number, which are the first three digits of your telephone number. This information will assist the Setup Wizard in providing you with the most efficient and least expensive access number. This number can be changed later by using the Settings button (see Setting Up Your Modem on page 4). Click Connect to continue.
5. When you are connected, MSN will download, or transfer to your computer, the latest software, product and pricing information, and an updated list of access phone numbers. It will then disconnect you, allowing you to fill in the necessary registration information off-line.

Installation Using the Set Up the Microsoft Network Icon

1. Double-click the Set Up the Microsoft Network icon.
2. Make sure the Yes, install the Microsoft Network button is selected and click OK. You may be prompted to install your original CD-ROM or diskette in the proper drive.
3. Fill in your country's location, your area code, any number you need to access an outside line (if necessary), and your touch-tone or pulse (rotary) dialing status. Click OK to continue.
4. The next window gives you a brief introduction to the Microsoft Network and verifies that you are not already an MSN member (Figure 1.12). Click OK to continue.
5. Fill in the next window. Your area code should already be filled in; add to it your local exchange number, which is the first three digits of your telephone number. This information will assist the Setup Wizard in providing you with the most efficient and least expensive access number. This number can be changed later by using the Settings button (see Setting Up Your Modem on page 4). Click Connect to continue.
6. When you are connected, MSN will download, or transfer to your computer, the latest software, product and pricing information, and an updated list of access phone numbers. It will then disconnect you, allowing you to fill in the necessary registration information off-line.

Registering with the Microsoft Network

By now you are probably anxious to begin. Your modem and software are installed, updated, and ready. All that's left is registration. If you have the Join Now window (Figure 1.13), skip to step 6, below.

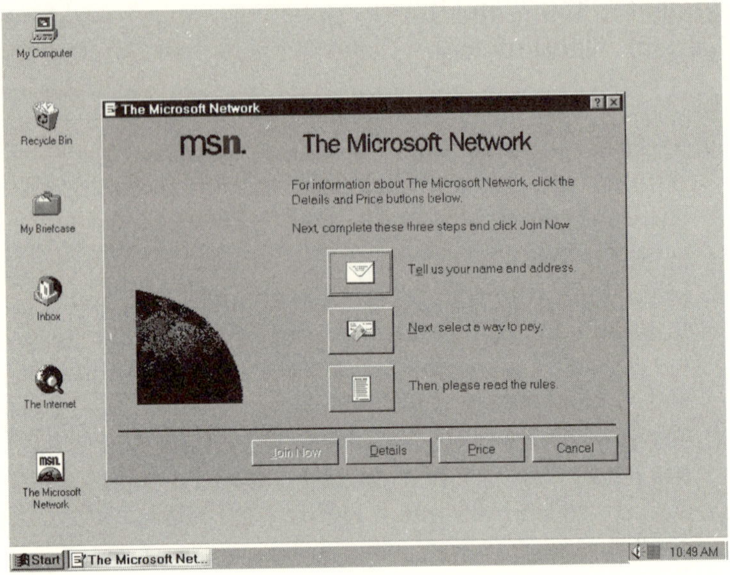

Figure 1.13 *Tell the Microsoft Network who you are and how you'll be paying, and you* must *read the rules.*

1. Double-click the MSN icon on the desktop.
2. Click the Yes button on your Invitation to Join the Microsoft Network. Doing this will start the registration process.
3. Fill in your area code and the first three digits of your telephone number.
4. The MSN software will return with local calling numbers for your particular area. If none can be found, it will try to select the closest ones. Because of local phone charges or problems in the telephone system, the number selected may not be the best choice. If it is not, click the Change button to select a number that will give you more favorable rates or better service. These numbers may be changed later if your needs change.

5. Click the Connect button. The MSN software will now access your modem and automatically dial the Microsoft Network to begin the on-line part of the registration process.
6. Next, you must tell MSN who you are and your method of payment. You must also read the rules. In addition, there are Details and Price buttons (Figure 1.13) that provide pricing and additional general information on the network.
7. Click the Envelope button to move to the name and address screen (Figure 1.14). Notice the check box on the lower left. Checking the box is a way of informing Microsoft and other organizations on the network that you do not wish to receive any information on their

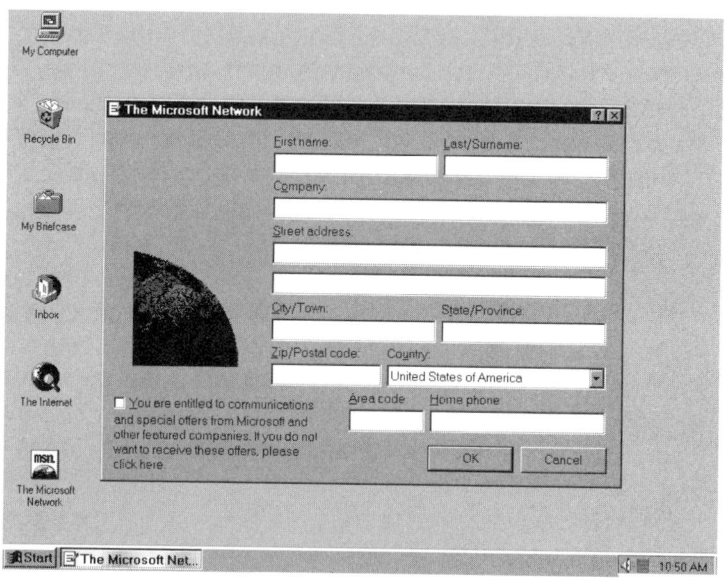

Figure 1.14 *Although you furnish the Microsoft Network with personal information, you can specify that it not be passed on to others.*

products and offerings. Receiving information in this way can be very helpful, as it is so hard to keep up with all that is going on in this changing world!

Using the Tab key, fill in the necessary information, then click OK to return to the previous screen.

Microsoft has elected to conform to the European privacy laws. What this means to you is that MSN's membership list may not be bought and sold, as so many other lists are. Each time you register for a service, you will be asked again if information may be sent to you. Independent content providers must also conform to these rules, sending you information on their products, but not selling the list to others.

8. Click the button with the picture of a credit card. Using the scroll bar if necessary, highlight the card you wish to use for payment. Your monthly charge will automatically appear on your regular credit card statement. Using the Tab key to move between fields, enter your credit card number, expiration date, and name on the card. When finished, click the OK button to return to the previous screen.

For those of you who are worried about credit card fraud, your credit card number is kept by MSN in a highly encrypted form. The same security measures are taken as when a retail merchant takes your card number. In fact, the credit card number is authorized through the same credit card network used when you make a standard purchase.

9. The last must-do item is to read the rules. Click the bottom button.

   By clicking the I Agree button (which you must do to move on), you accept all of Microsoft's terms and conditions for MSN.

10. After returning to the first sign-up screen, which you do by clicking the I Agree button, take a little time to browse through some of the additional information available to you. Click the Details button to see the latest information about MSN (which may have been just downloaded to your computer).
11. Next, press the Price button. Review the information to make sure you understand the MSN pricing structure and its various options.
12. Click the Join Now button. The next window presents you with the access phone numbers that MSN has determined are best for your location. Click the Change button to review your choices, as you may find a number much closer to you than the software did! Make any necessary changes and Click OK to return to the first phone number window.
13. Click OK to continue, then Connect to finish the registration process.
14. Type in what you would like to use as a member ID. This is the name you will be known by on the network. It is a good idea to choose an ID that is unique to you, avoiding such IDs as Steve_G or A_Smith. Microsoft doesn't care if you use your real name or make up a new identity, so you can choose anything you want (subject to the usual limits of good taste). These IDs are not case sensitive. BarneyF will get you to the same place as barneyf.

Although you can choose a "new identity," it can only be from your imagination. You may not under any circumstances represent yourself as someone you are not.

Although you can change your member ID, it cannot be done on-line. For security reasons, to change your ID you must call the Customer Service in your region. For information on regional phone numbers, see the following When Things Go Wrong section.

15. Type in your password. Your password must be between 8 and 16 characters long. This is the equivalent to a PIN on a credit or bank card and should be guarded closely.

Congratulations! You are now a member of The Microsoft Network. An icon in the shape of the MSN logo is now on your desktop (Figure 1.15). Click the Finish button.

Chapter 2 will lead you through actually signing on and the rudiments of MSN navigation. Or, if you've been successful so far, double-click the MSN icon on your desktop, fill in your ID and password, click connect, and get started!

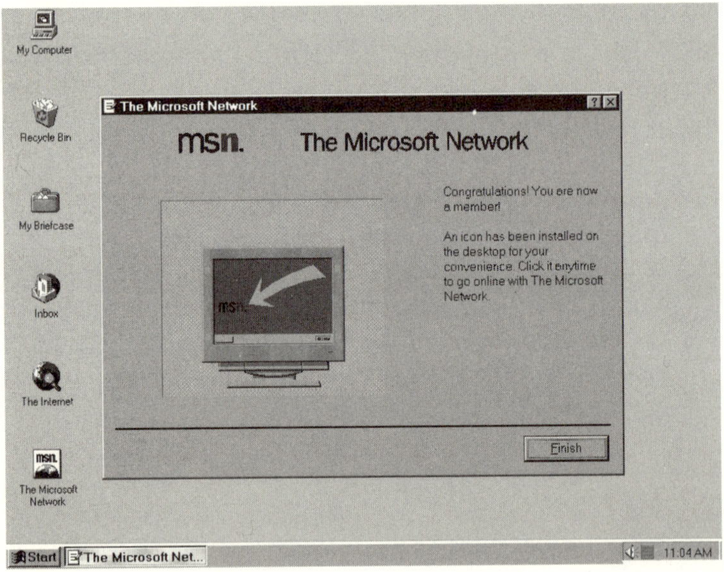

Figure 1.15 *Congratulations! At last you are a member, and the software installation is complete.*

When Things Go Wrong

If you are having trouble connecting, take advantage of Microsoft's excellent Help feature. This will lead you, no matter what the problem, to a resolution.

1. Click the task bar Start button and select Help.
2. Click the Index tab at the top of the Help window.
3. As the words to look up, type **Microsoft Network**.
4. Highlight the words "connecting to," located right beneath "Microsoft Network on-line service."
5. Click the Display button.
6. The next dialog box, Figure 1.16, will lead you to the actual troubleshooting process. Click on the small box (Related Topics) on the bottom left to begin.

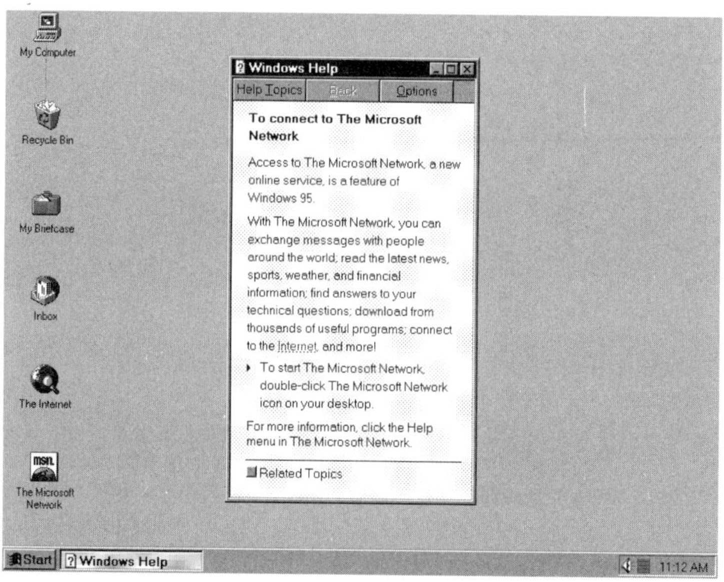

Figure 1.16 *If you are experiencing difficulties connecting to the Microsoft Network, Help is never far away.*

7. On the list will be "Troubleshooting MSN sign-up and access problems."
8. Click Display. You will be presented with the options shown in Figure 1.17. Select the one that pertains to your situation. Each successive dialog box (you'll get different ones depending on which selections you make) will either lead you to try a possible solution or direct you to close Help because you have solved the problem!

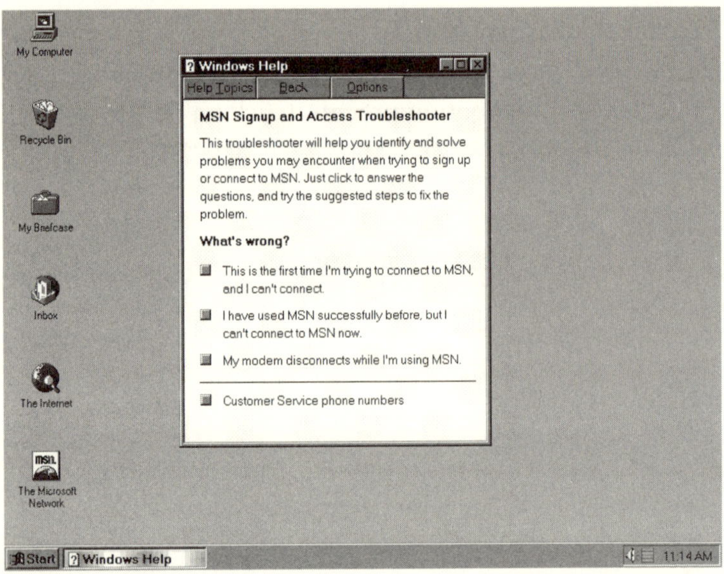

Figure 1.17 *The more questions you answer about the nature of the problem in Help, the more specific the questions or recommendations become.*

9. Finally, if all else fails, the last Help window, shown in Figure 1.18, provides member support phone numbers. Scroll through the list until you find your calling area. These phone numbers are for technical support, and a live person can then walk you through any further troubleshooting.

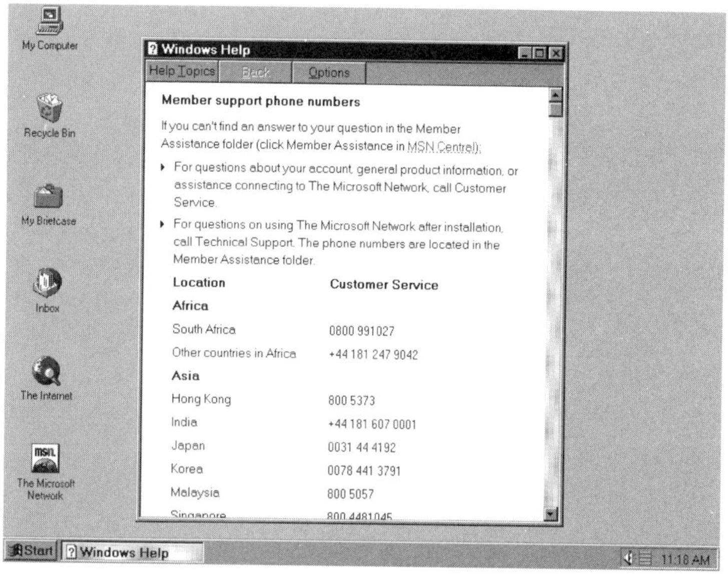

Figure 1.18 *If Help cannot solve your problem, regional phone numbers, with real people, are available worldwide.*

CHAPTER 2

Signing On and Off and Using Pull-Down Menus

OK, you've been reading about all the neat things and places to see that are awaiting you, and you've gone through all the installation and registration steps and are now a bona fide registered member of the Microsoft Network. What now?

In this chapter you'll learn how extraordinarily easy it is to sign on, sign off, and make MSN behave the way that's best for you. You'll also learn some basics for getting around and finding what you need and where you need to go. As mentioned previously, if you are at all familiar with Windows 95, you'll feel right at home with MSN.

I've been telling you about communicating with like-minded people all over the world, making financial transactions, discovering answers to virtually any question, finding friends, and playing games. If it still seems a little intimidating, don't worry! We'll do some free-form exploring and find our way back home again.

Logging On for the First Time

If you have finished the registration procedure described in Chapter 1, you are ready to really begin, sign on, and get going. If not, Chapter 1 gives a full description of the registration process.

1. Double-click the MSN icon on your desktop. This will bring up the log-on screen (Figure 2.1).

If you did not do the MSN software installation yourself, click the Settings... button before trying to connect for the first time and check that the default settings are the right ones for your situation. Of course, if you've just finished the installation yourself you probably do not need to check the settings. In the future, if the computer is a desktop one or otherwise in a consistently stable environment, you certainly do not need to check this every time. For more information on Settings refer to Chapter 1.

---

2. Type in your password. As you type, asterisks appear instead of the actual characters. This prevents any busybodies who may be close by from merely looking over your shoulder to discover your secret log-on code.
3. The check box under the word "Password" in Figure 2.1 gives the option of having your password entered automatically each time you log on. Be very careful with this option. It will enable anyone with access to your computer to use the Microsoft Network, and all its member services, as though they were you!

This option is only available if your computer uses passwords to sign on to Windows 95. If the selection and the selection box is grayed out, you will need to set up separate user passwords for each of the people who use your system. From the Start menu, select Settings, Control Panel, and finally Passwords.

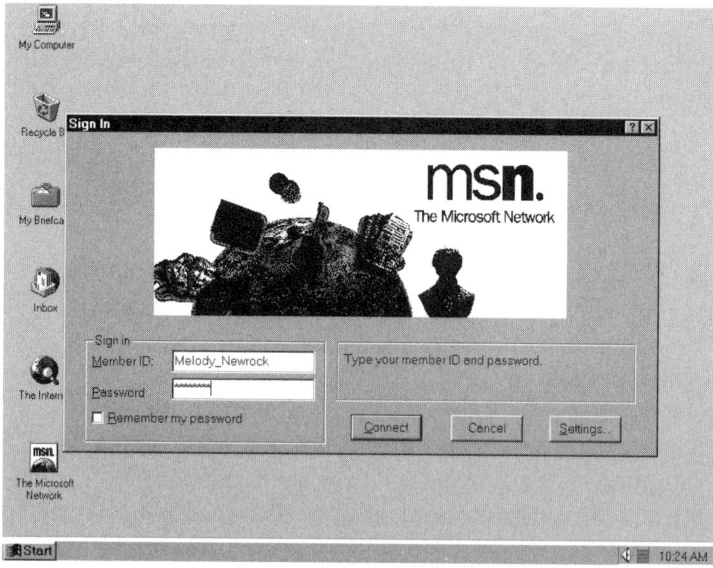

Figure 2.1 *The Microsoft Network Sign In screen where you enter your Member ID and password.*

4. Click the Connect button.

Wait while the MSN software dials the Microsoft Network using your modem. If you have an external modem, you will first hear a dial tone and then the number being dialed. On the front of the modem, lights will flash, indicating that the phone is Off Hook (OH) and when the modem is Receiving Data (RD) or Sending Data (SD). With an internal modem, these sounds will not be so apparent (but you may be able to hear them) and there will obviously be no flashing lights! With either type of modem you'll hear a rough, hissing sound as the modem makes the connection.

As the connection is made, notice the small modem icon that appears on the right side of the task bar, next to the volume control icon. On the modem icon there are two tiny red lights that flash to green as data is transferred back and forth. If you rest your mouse cursor on the modem icon, you'll see how many bytes have been sent and received. To the right of the modem icon is another small icon, the MSN Indicator, indicating you are using the Microsoft Network.

Welcome aboard!

MSN Today

MSN Today is the default screen you will see each time you log on to MSN. Here you will find news of upcoming events, including live questions and answer sessions with people foremost in their fields. It will introduce additional features, such as new forums or navigational techniques. It may even tell you about things you may have missed, such as ongoing mystery series that are updated weekly. (In case you first learn of them at installment 32, they come complete with "back issues.")

More than just giving information from all over the globe, MSN Today gives you the correct times and dates and/or direct routes to these fascinating places. For example, clicking the time of the event in Figure 2.2 brings a list with the correct time for all local time zones. Then, clicking the graphic associated with the event automatically transports you to where you need to be!

In fact, just as in all Windows Help environments, clicking on text that appears in a different color and/or is underlined will always bring more information.

On the left is a list of other features available from MSN, each one a selectable item. Click on Calendar of Events and get a complete list of upcoming forums, live chats, and special meetings. You can also choose Member Assistance for some quick tips on the Microsoft Network itself or Go Words to move quickly out and to another area. This list is ever changing and expanding, another reason to check out MSN Today on a regular basis.

Figure 2.2 *MSN Today is where you instantly find out what's new, current, and relevant on the Microsoft Network.*

As informative as it is, it MSN Today can be graphically intensive and, as a result, slow to draw the screen. If you don't have the patience for this feature each and every time you sign on, you can prevent it from opening when you sign on to MSN, but still be able to retrieve it at will. Following the directions given below allows you to bypass MSN Today on opening, and then bring it up at will.

All Aboard MSN Central

MSN Central (Figure 2.3), like the great railroad stations of yesterday, is where you will start your sojourns into the wide, wide world of on-line networking. Here you will start customizing your on-line environment, plumping up the cushions in your first-class coach if you will. With these five starting points, you can get anywhere, see anything, and get whatever help you need. Each one is really just a large button to click. Let's briefly look at the five main options, one at a time. In later chapters we will begin examining each one in much greater depth.

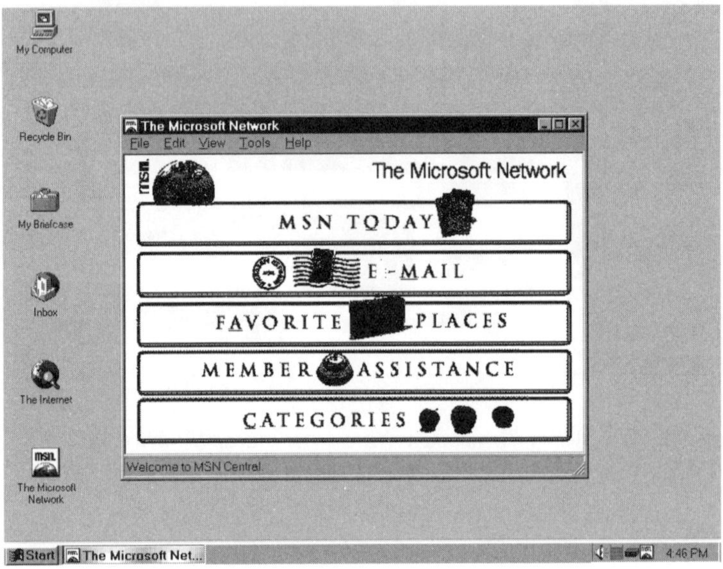

Figure 2.3 *MSN Central is your gateway to all the Microsoft Network services.*

Try right-clicking on the Connection Indicator, the MSN icon located on the task bar next to the time. A menu appears with several options, including View MSN Central (to quickly return here from other MSN areas). Other options are Send Mail, Go To, View Favorite Places, and Sign Out.

MSN Today

If you've decided you do not want the MSN Today screen to come up automatically each time you log on, or if you just need to get back to it, simply click on this option.

E-Mail

Perhaps more than any other, E-Mail is the feature that brings people to on-line services. It is a powerful, exciting communication tool, allowing you to send messages instantly not only to other MSN subscribers, but also to people on other services such as CompuServe and Prodigy. And it doesn't stop there. If you know people's Internet addresses, E-Mail them there!

Favorite Places

As you explore your new environment, you will find yourself returning to places of special interest with greater and greater frequency. Perhaps research is your thing and Microsoft Encarta, an on-line encyclopedia, finds you a recurrent visitor. Rather than moving down through screen after screen, or typing Go words, add the encyclopedia as well as any other tools or places you often visit to your own personal Favorite Places area.

Member Assistance

We all need a little help sometime in life! While Member Assistance can't solve the problems of what to make for dinner or what to get your employees for Christmas (you'll have to get those answers from other areas on MSN), it can make your trip into this unfamiliar territory of MSN much more enjoyable and productive. Here you will not only find out how to get around and do things, but you will also find information on accepted ways to behave—commonly referred to as *Netiquette*—and member guidelines.

Check out the MSN Member Lobby (Figure 2.4). Here you will find Maps and Information, which includes regularly scheduled introductory tours of MSN, a Reception

Desk, and the Member Directory. Here is where you can meet new members or practice using MSN with special tools that you can use to find particular areas of interest without having to worry about making mistakes.

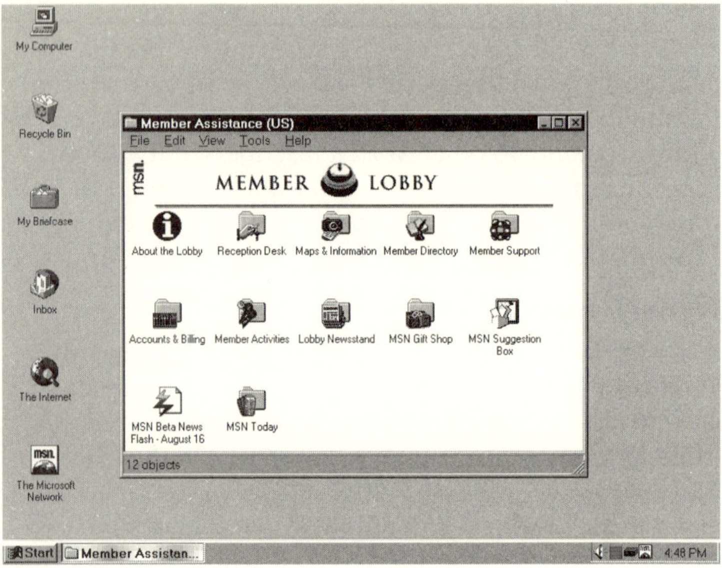

Figure 2.4 *The Member Lobby has different areas to address any aspect of your membership or the Microsoft Network itself.*

If your questions cannot be addressed using the on-line Help, Member Support has a Help Desk that contains all the top questions about all aspects of MSN, and if your question is not there, a place is provided for it.

There's still more in the MSN Member Lobby. Visit the gift shop to purchase MSN-related books, T-shirts, and other merchandise. And don't forget to keep up to date vis-à-vis the latest special promotions, contests, activities, and MSN-related news.

Categories

Categories is where our trip will really begin. Clicking on Categories takes us to the heart of MSN, to the folders and files of user groups and newsgroups, bulletin boards and chat rooms, auditoriums and shopping trips. Be prepared to spend some time here, as you never know what you'll find on any given day. New features, forums, and content providers are added every day, so check regularly and you may find your Favorite Places filling up fast!

If you find that you've lost track of time, don't worry. Double-click the modem icon and you'll see just how long you've been connected (Figure 2.5).

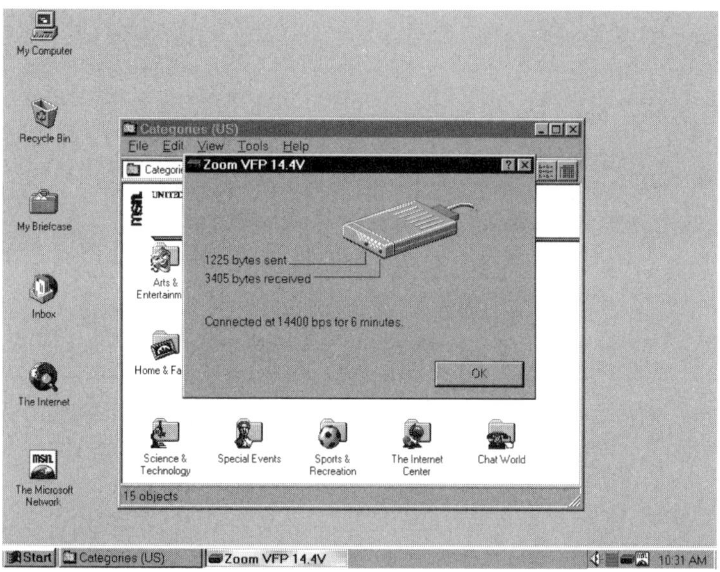

Figure 2.5 *Double-click the modem mini icon on the task bar to keep yourself apprised of connect time.*

Pull-Down Menus

Like other Windows programs, MSN makes extensive use of pull-down menus. What follows here is a brief discussion of the five that you see at the top of MSN Central. Keep in mind that when you are using other parts of MSN, such as chat areas, E-Mail, and forums, there may be other, additional pull-down menus. Even within these five, there may be additional menu items. These additions will be discussed as we see them and need them.

If you look at the menu list at the top of the screen, you'll see some very familiar pull-down menu names: File, Edit, View, Tools, and Help. Very familiar names, but some surprises await you when you pull them down.

File

Click the File menu and you'll find Up One Level, Sign In, Sign Out, and Close. You will find that the File menu options, in fact all menu options, will change as you change your location on MSN. As we journey further, a lot of these tools will be discussed. But don't forget that the best way to find your way is to just dig in and try to use all the new and different resources Microsoft makes available.

Just as in Windows, it is not always necessary to use the mouse. By holding down the Alt key at the same time as the underlined letter of the menu you need, then of the underlined character of the specific menu item, you will be taken where you want to go. For example, pressing the Alt key at the same time as the letter F will pull down the File menu; by then pressing the letter T, you can sign out.

- Just as you might suspect, Up One Level takes you back to MSN Today. Up One Level will always do just that, take you back to where you were last, in this case MSN Today.

- Sign Out logs you off, after presenting you with the disconnect confirmation screen.
- Close accomplishes the same thing as clicking the X in the upper-right corner of the screen. The topmost window closes, and the ones underneath (if you have more than one window open at a time) move up.

As you can see, just as in Windows 95, there are always at least two ways to do anything. And we haven't even gotten to toolbars yet!

Edit

Let's move on to Edit, where the pull down menu reveals, Go To▸. Moving the mouse to the right as indicated by the ▸symbol reveals your choices, in this case MSN Central, which is grayed out as you are already there, Favorite Places, and Other Locations.

1. To find out a specific service's Go word, first highlight the service's icon, then pull down the File menu. One of the menu options will be Properties.
2. Click on Properties, to find general information about the service (Figure 2.6), including its Go word. There are yet still different ways to get to a service, but this is one of the quickest.

View

The View menu allows you to customize your screen. The four options are Toolbar, Status Bar, Refresh, and Options.

- Click on Toolbar and a second bar appears, just under the current menu bar. This second bar contains many useful icons and navigation tools (Figure 2.7).

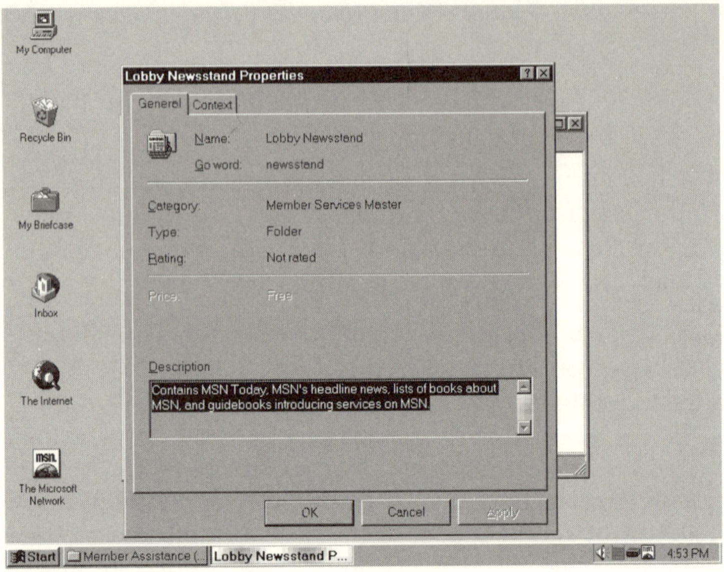

Figure 2.6 *An icon's Properties box offers up a wealth of information about a feature, including its Go Word to get you back in a hurry.*

Figure 2.7 *Adding a toolbar steps up the pace of navigating the network. A window can be resized to add the now necessary space.*

First and largest on the left is a scroll menu. Click on the right-hand down arrow and you will get a list in a tree-type structure of different folders you can jump right to. As you learn your way around, this method will save you a considerable amount of time. While you may not know a location's Go word or want to use the Find feature, skimming around the folders in this way is much quicker than navigating full-screen folders and icons!

To the right of the scroll bar are various icons. All of these icons will appear and work the same way, wherever you are in MSN. In other words, the folder with the up arrow will always move you up one level, from where you just came. The next icon, a small building, brings you back to MSN Central, the icon with a folder with a star on it is your Favorite Places, and, last, the cross-hatch icon signs you off.

- Next on the View menu is Status Bar. When this is checked (meaning it's been selected) a bar on the bottom of the current window reminds you of where you are on MSN.
- Refresh updates your screen. Due to time delays, your screen may not have the most up-to-the-minute information. Refresh takes care of the problem.
- Options lets you change the way MSN actually looks and behaves. Click on Options and notice the tabs at the top: View, File Types, General, and Folder. For now we will look only at General and Folder.

Click on General (Figure 2.8), and change the amount of time that has to pass with no action on your part before you are automatically disconnected. You may enter a number between 1 and 59 for the number of minutes.

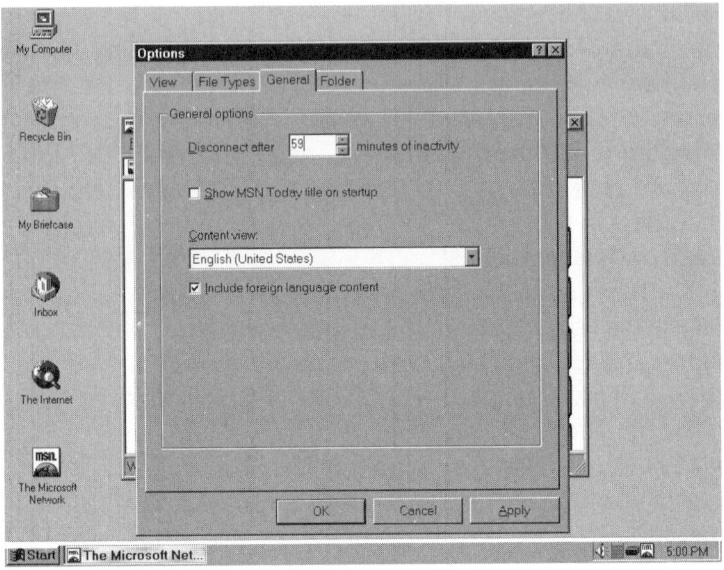

Figure 2.8 *Use Options to configure the Microsoft Network to your specifications.*

Keep in mind that if you use Help extensively, or spend a lot of time composing and reading mail or bulletin board messages while on-line, MSN will not notice any activity because you will be working from your hard disk. Before you know it, up will pop a dialog box asking you to confirm that it is OK for you to be disconnected, and off you'll go.

The other item of interest here is the check box for determining whether the MSN Central screen appears automatically each time you log on. Check the box only if you *do* want it to show up.

Next let's look at Folder (Figure 2.9). Each time you select a task in MSN a window with that particular task is opened. Before long, if you don't keep up with closing them, you've got an awful lot of windows open on your desktop. This is not only annoying, but it will also gobble up all your resources as well. It *is* handy to be able to jump from window to window, but after a time, depending on how you use MSN, you may decide it is better to have the windows close as you move about. Doing so will limit your viewing to one folder at a time, but you may find that using the Up One Level icon or the scroll bar is a better alternative.

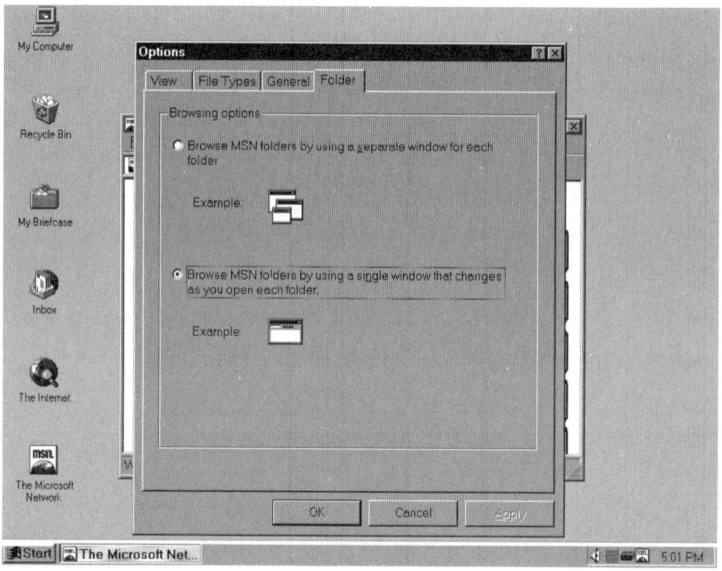

Figure 2.9 *The Options Folder tab where you tell MSN how many folders to leave on while navigating the network.*

Tools

The Tools menu has the nuts and bolts of what you need to get the most out of MSN and to keep track of how much it's costing you! The available options are Find, Password, Billing, File Transfer Status, and Connection Settings.

Using Find to Locate Particular Services Find presents you with three more choices: Files or Folders, Computer, and On the Microsoft Network. Files or Folders will check your computer, looking for a file you specify by name, date modified, or other criteria such as specific text or particular size. Of course, if you are on a network and your computer is not where the file is, this feature will not be of much help. That's where the Computer selection comes in handy. Select the computer you need to search in, and then go to Files or Folders.

On the Microsoft Network is really what we are concerned with here. You know you've seen it—that thing you're looking for—somewhere in your travels, but where? A wonderful forum, or bulletin board, or anything, and you can't remember where! There are literally hundreds and hundreds of likely paths and possibilities, so it's not too hard to lose track of where you've been.

1. Click the On the Microsoft Network selection.
2. When the box shown in Figure 2.10 appears in the input box called Containing, type in the word you think comes closest to the subject you are looking for.

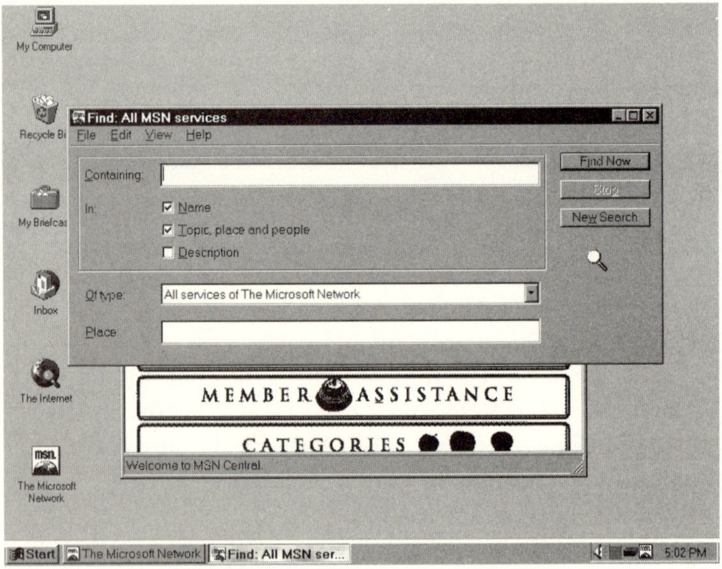

Figure 2.10 *Using Find you can locate virtually any service available on the Microsoft Network.*

3. The three check boxes underneath let you limit the search further. Should the word be in the name, be the topic, be just the description, or all three?
4. Click on the down arrow in the Of Type box. Take a look at the options available to you regarding where you define the type of services, such as only bulletin boards or chat rooms, or all services, including MSN and the Internet. Select On the Microsoft Network.
5. The Place box is where you can specify a particular geographic area in relation to your topic. If you are planning a trip to New York, you could enter **New York,** or **New,** or **York** or **new york** for that matter.

Find will allow you to use standard DOS wildcard conventions, the * and ? characters. Use the * for more than one character at the end of a search string, such as net* to find nets or netting. Use the ? at the beginning of a search string, as a substitute for only one character. For example, a search for **?et** will find net, nets, netting and bet, bets or betting.

Find also supports the use of the words "and" and "or." You can search for "books and library" to get a list that contains both words, or "books or library" to get a list that contains either word.

---

6. Click the Find Now button and wait a short time while the list is compiled. When it is finished, you will have a list in the bottom half of the window (Figure 2.11), specifying the name of the location, what type it is (folder, chat, bulletin board, for example), the size, and when it was last modified. The Find list is limited (!?) to 500 entries, so you may find that you have to narrow your search somewhat at times.
7. Best of all, just double-click on the item you want, and off you go! No need to return to MSN Central, use Go words, find Categories and work your way down, or anything else. If you need to see more information before moving on, right-click the item, and click Properties.

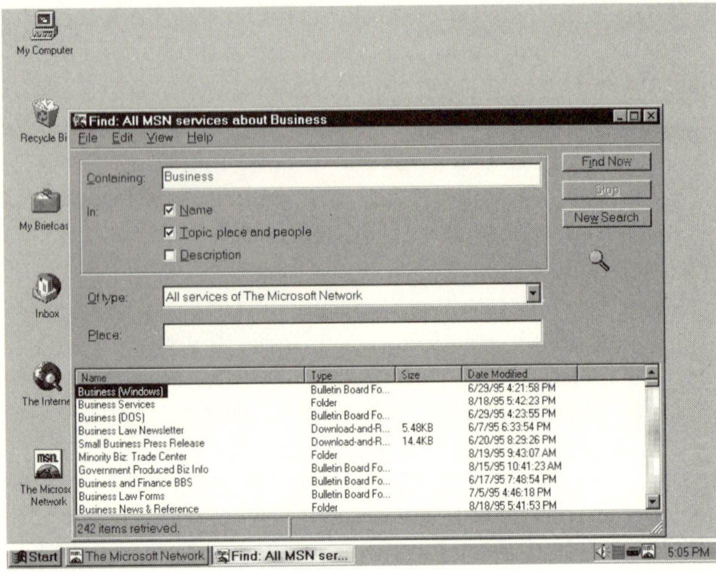

Figure 2.11 *Find gives a complete list of all the services located.*

Your list may contain what appears to be duplicate entries. When a forum manager creates a link to a service, the link shows up in Find. When many different forum managers create links to the same service, they all show up in Find. Of course, there is also the possibility that different forum managers may use the same name for different services!

Changing Your Password The next item in the Tools menu is Password. Just as you might suspect, it is here where you change your current password.

1. Pull down the Tools menu, and select Password.
2. Type in your current password (Figure 2.12). Just as when you originally signed on, only asterisks (*) appear as you type.

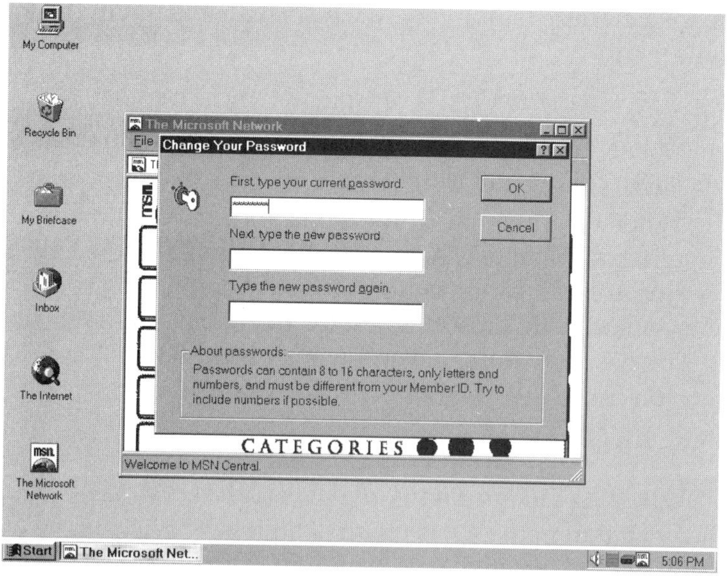

Figure 2.12 *To prevent access to sensitive information, it helps to change your password on a regular basis.*

3. Type in a new password. Again, it must be more than eight characters, and don't make it too easy to remember or someone else may figure it out!
4. In the next box, repeat the process. Because all you see are asterisks, you need to confirm that this is really your choice. If you had made a typing error and did not type what you had intended, you would not otherwise know of the error and would have a password unknown even to you.
5. Click the OK button and wait for the confirmation box to appear.

Billing Although the basic connect time charge is very reasonable, there always seems to be something else to spend money on. MSN allows you to have complete oversight of your monthly charges and provides payment flexibility. These billing tools are also available under the Tools menu.

Changing Credit Cards and Other Billing Information

1. Pull down the Tools menu, Select Billing, and then click on Payment Method.
2. When the Payment Options box appears, click on the envelope icon to change your billing name and address or the credit card icon to change the credit card you would like Microsoft to use for payment. These screens are basically the same ones you entered data into when you first joined MSN.
3. Click OK to finish.

Retrieving On-line Billing and Subscription Statements

The next item in the Tools menu is Billing. This is a very useful feature. From the moment you first sign on, you will find that the expression "time flies" has a whole new meaning. MSN gives you the ability to monitor both your time and how much you've spent.

Summary of Charges

1. Pull down the Tools menu and select Billing.
2. Make sure the Statement tab at the top of the window is on top (Figure 2.13).
3. You will see four blank columns: Date, Description, Amount, and Total.
4. Click the Get Details button.

A dialog box asks you for the period you need to focus on: current or previous months. Highlight the time you need and you'll return to the previous screen, this time with all the columns filled in, in order by date, along with your current balance and any free connect time you may still have left for the period. Payments and credits are shown as negative numbers. These are actual usage charges, which are calculated by actual time spent on line.

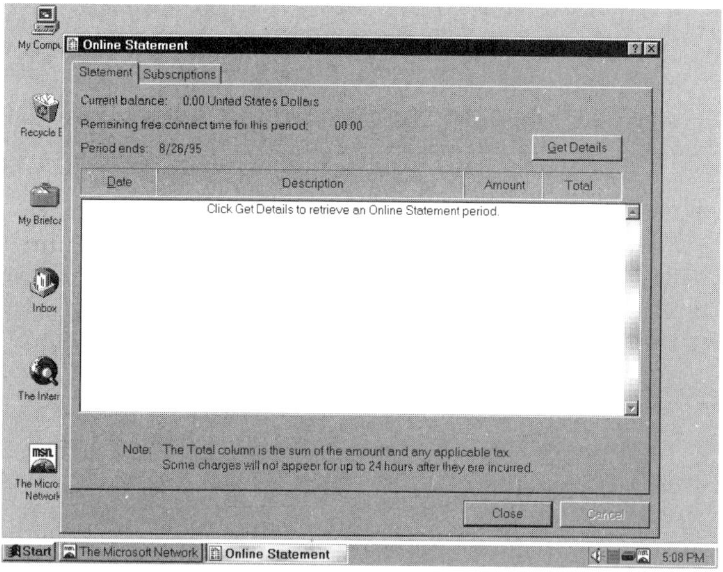

Figure 2.13 *Keep track of all your current charges using the On-line Statement.*

The Billing Statement box also keeps you apprised of any other costs you have incurred. This includes electronic files you have downloaded for which there was a charge, special events in auditoriums, and any chat rooms or forums with cover charges. You would have been made aware of any charges associated with these last items at the time of the transactions.

Subscriptions Subscriptions pertain to areas of MSN for which you are billed separately by an independent content provider (ICP). For instance, an ICP may offer a series of forums on-line, for which there is no extra charge. But for those who would like to receive more specific or significant information, such as reports, special offers, or access to particular people not available to the general public, a subscription would be offered at an additional charge.

1. If you are currently in the Billing Statement window, click the Subscription tab at the top. Or, if you are not in the Billing Statement window, pull down the Tools menu, select Billing, the click on Subscriptions.
2. The top window in Figure 2.14 lists all current subscriptions and any associated credits on your account. The bottom window offers a more detailed description of the highlighted plan in the top window.

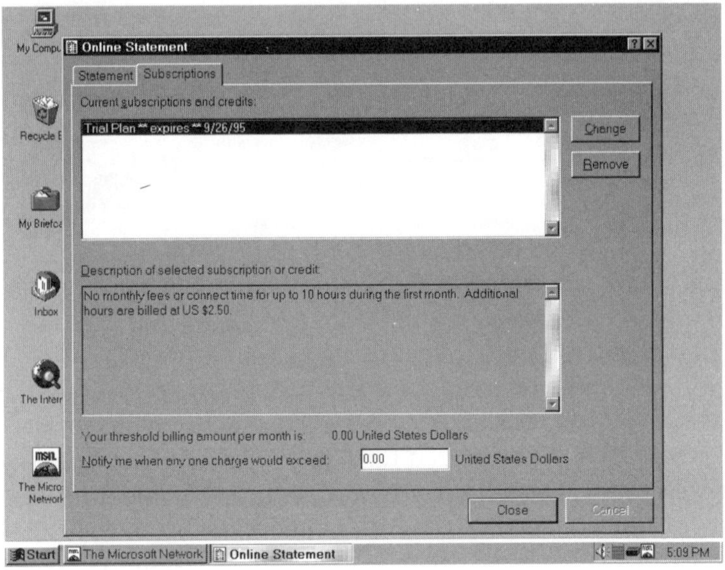

Figure 2.14 *Subscriptions can be easily changed or removed with the click of a mouse.*

3. To make a change, select a plan by highlighting it in the top window. Click the Change button for alternate subscription plans.
4. To change your plan, simply select the new plan by highlighting it, then click the OK button.

5. Finally, you will be asked to verify that you wish to make the change. Click OK and the new subscription will be sent to MSN.

Canceling Membership If you find that you must cancel your membership, you cannot do so on-line but must call Customer Service. All current member support numbers for your region can be found in the Help menu.

File Transfer Status There will be many occasions for you to transfer large files. MSN E-Mail and other types of messaging allow you to attach files to be sent along with the original communication. Or perhaps you need to download program files, either freeware or shareware, or even full-size programs commercially available for sale. At some point after the beginning of the transfer from the MSN server to your computer, these files are placed in a transfer queue. From the Tools menu, you can view the status of the files.

Along with the name of the file you will see its size, time sent, current status in delivery, and the destination on your hard drive. You choose the destination by selecting Options under the Tools menu in the File Transfer Status window. The File Transfer Status window is discussed in more detail in Chapter 7, on bulletin boards.

Connection Settings The last item in the Tools menu is Connection Settings. This is the same series of Connection Settings dialog boxes we reviewed in the previous chapter. At any time during your MSN sessions, you can check the settings and make changes to either the Access Numbers, Dialing Properties, or Modem Settings.

Help

The last item on this first, introductory menu is Help. Because MSN's Help feature is so extensive, it deserves a chapter of its own, following this one. Chapter 3 is a practical, hands-on guide to the entire Help system, including what to do if you are having trouble accessing MSN in the first place!

CHAPTER 3

Getting and Using Help

Ever since Windows 3.1, Microsoft has provided excellent Help features, and the Microsoft Network is no exception. In fact, Windows 95 and MSN expand considerably the Help options available to you, while maintaining ease of use. After all, what good are Help features if you can't figure out how to use them?

Despite its comprehensiveness, the Help menu has only three items: Help Topics, Member Support Numbers, and About the Microsoft Network.

Help Topics is where you go when you are unsure how to do something on MSN. It is a very extensive Help system, often leading you by the hand in step-by-step procedures. It is a good place to browse occasionally, as you would a printed encyclopedia. You will discover how to do things you never thought of doing in the first place, and will wonder how you did without such know-how!

Help Table of Contents

After selecting Help Topics from the Help menu, you'll see three tabs at the top of the Help Topics window: Contents, which will be on top and selected, Index, and Find. Contents is where the broadest of categories are set out, such as Introducing The Microsoft Network, How To..., Tips and Tricks, and Troubleshooting (Figure 3.1). When you are unsure of where to even begin looking, this is a good place to start.

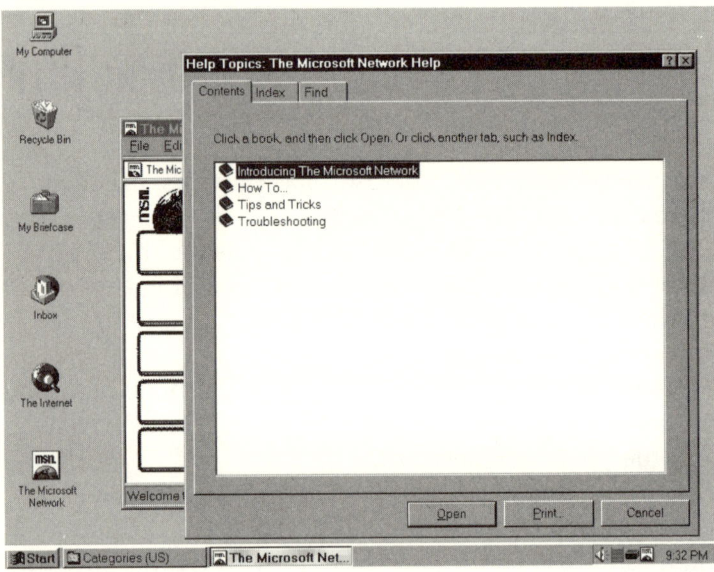

Figure 3.1 *The Microsoft Network Help system is extensive. Start out with this general Table of Contents.*

You do not have to be on-line to peruse Help. If you have a long list of topics to look up, or just feel like browsing, don't waste valuable connect time. When you do anticipate a long Help session, bring up Help while you are on-line and then sign out. Help will remain behind, fully featured and ready to use.

Using the Help Index

If you have an idea of the nature of the problem, or at least have a general idea of what the name of the process is that you are looking for, click the Index tab. For example, suppose you want to add new E-Mail addresses to your personal Electronic Mail address book. By typing **add** as the word you are looking for, Help takes you to the heading "adding," and under this heading is a long list of different things that can be added to, including "addresses to your personal address book." Had you typed in **address** you would have been taken straight to the heading "address book," under which is a long list of appropriate Help topics (Figure 3.2). This time, though, they all pertain to your personal on-line address book.

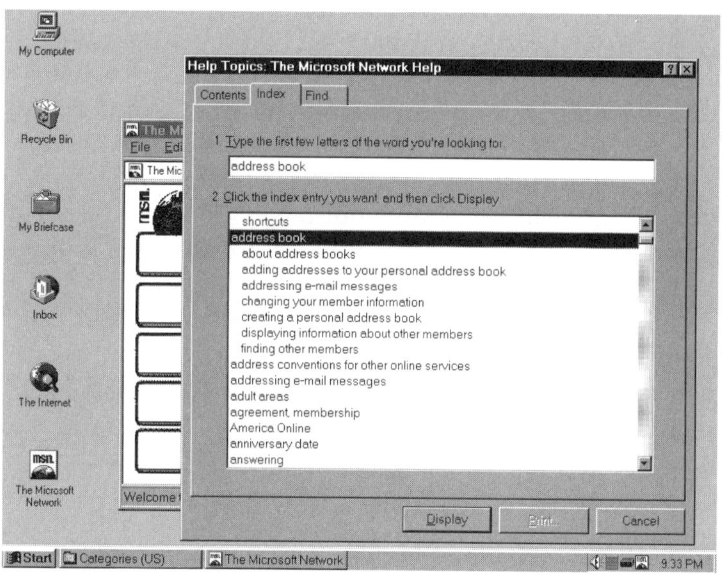

Figure 3.2 *Using the Help Index, enter a word and select from the displayed list the topic you need.*

Help and Find

The last tab, Find, is a little trickier. If you cannot get the help you need because no Help Topic categories seem relevant to the task at hand, you will have to use the Find tab. Instead of relying on subject heads and categories, Find looks for particular words, sentences, or phrases within the Help Topic itself.

For example, suppose you needed to change one of your subscriptions. If you were to type the word **change** using the Help Index tab, you would find that there are no categories starting with the word "change." Yet you still need to find how to change your subscriptions.

1. Click the Find tab.
2. Make sure the Minimize database size button is selected (Figure 3.3). This is the recommended approach because it usually gets the job done in the least amount of time. Selecting the Maximize search capabilities button will enlarge the list of words to search on, but it may take considerably longer not only to build the list, but also to get the final result.

   The Customize search button gives the option of selecting files to search. Among them are MSN Internet Help, MSN Mail Help, and Common Help. Bear in mind that nothing is final! After creating the list, you can always go back and Rebuild it.
3. With the Minimize database size button selected, click the Next button.
4. Now, click the Finish button. This may or may not take a lot of time. Be patient, it is well worth the wait.
5. Finally, you will see a window similar to the one in Figure 3.4. Click the Options button. Here you customize just how the Find function looks through the list of words you just created.

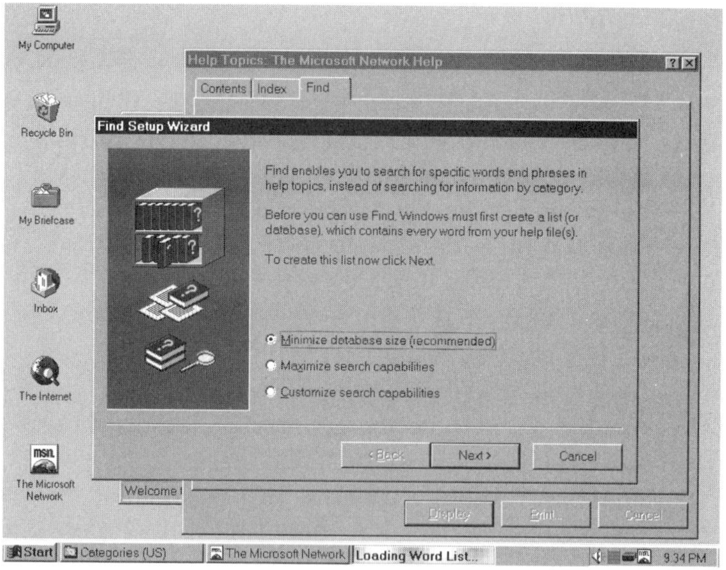

Figure 3.3 *Help has its own Find function to locate the Help Topic you are having trouble otherwise locating.*

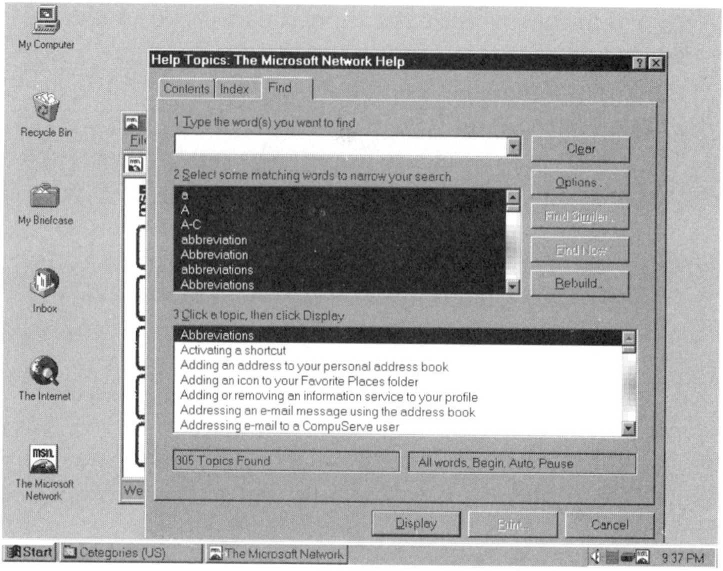

Figure 3.4 *The Help Find feature searches out every occurrence of a word or phrase until you see the one you need.*

- Pay careful attention to the search methods offered. You can instruct Find to look at the words you typed in exactly or to match with letters that may be within a larger word or phrase. Alternatively, should it find all the words typed in any order or only in the order in which you entered them? Make your choices, and if you have no luck in finding the topic you need, the Options button will always be there to make changes and try again.
- Finally, choose how soon after each keystroke the search shall begin. Immediately, or not until the Find Now button is clicked? This is pure personal preference. I prefer immediately as I sometimes catch sight of a topic along the way that I find interesting, and then make a detour.

6. Click OK to return to the Find window.
7. Now, simply type in words you are looking for. Let's return to the example mentioned earlier; you want to find out about changing subscriptions but there is no match for "change" using the Help Index tab. Type **change** in the Find window.

   Several matches were found! The top box lists each instance when the word "change" appears. By highlighting each one, you can see in the bottom box the particular Help Topic in which it appears: in this case (Figure 3.5), "Changing your payment method or billing information."
8. Click Display and all the information you need is at your fingertips!

Using this full complement of Help functions, you will be able to find your way around virtually any MSN problem.

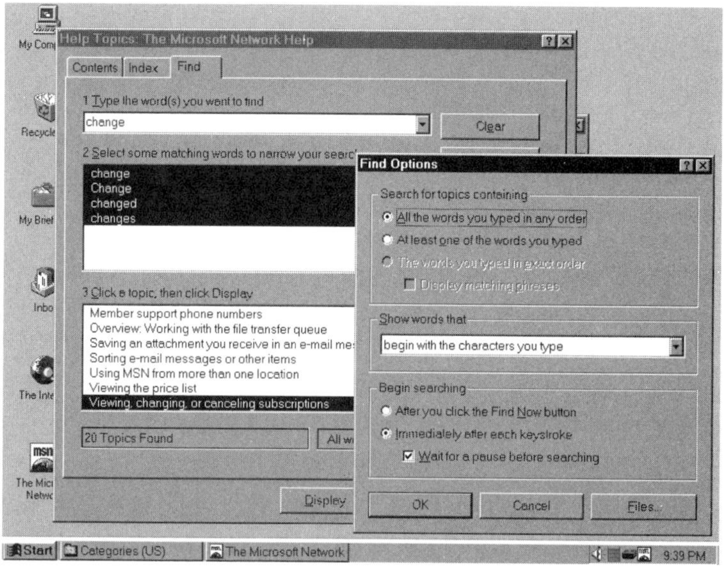

Figure 3.5 *The Help Find Options let you retrieve and display the results in a variety of ways.*

Most of the time you are offered the option of printing a Help Topic. For complicated procedures, or ones you may not use often and had difficulty finding, doing this is a good idea. After a time you will have put together your own personal MSN manual.

Experts at Your Fingertips

No matter whether you use the Index, Table of Contents, or Find, you will often find an "Expert" at your side to lead you through a problem. For, in addition to telling you how to solve problems, several areas of Help have Experts to troubleshoot specific, usually hardware-related questions. For example, if you're having trouble with your printer, the Help system will walk you through a troubleshooting analysis including test printing intended to isolate the nature of the problem.

MSN Support Numbers

For those times when nothing but a real person will do, such as changing certain member information and your account setup, support numbers are available. There are two ways to reach the regional area phone number list in MSN Help. One way is to select the second menu item on the Help menu, MSN Support Numbers.

However, after those rare times when you are led by Help through each step only to find that your problem has not been solved, Help automatically brings up the MSN Support phone number list as the step of last resort!

CHAPTER 4

Sending and Receiving E-Mail

Electronic mail has forever changed the way people communicate with each other. Most people in the computer business, on college campuses, and in large corporations check for messages at least daily, and frequently more often than that. E-Mail allows you to present complex ideas and forceful arguments quickly and efficiently. And unlike the Post Office (commonly referred to as Snail Mail), it gets your thoughts to their intended recipient instantly. While other quick means of communicating, like the telephone and voice mail, can result in a conversation that may not go as you intended or a message that may come across as hurried, E-Mail gets the message there with the tone of the communication *exactly* as you intended. And nothing beats E-Mail for communicating across different time zones, allowing you to reach overseas clients or colleagues promptly.

Microsoft Exchange, the engine that powers E-Mail on MSN, allows you to include graphics and attached files, specify fonts and colors, and even include shortcuts to other areas on MSN with your messages. After you have received your mail, you can instantly and automatically send a reply, or you forward it to someone else with attachments and a note of your own.

Microsoft Exchange works the way *you* do. Outgoing mail goes to your Outbox, and incoming mail to your Inbox. Your Inbox displays all your mail, whether it came from other MSN users, off the Internet, or from other services such as America Online or CompuServe.

This chapter takes you step by step through all of these Exchange features and more. Among them will be customizing your Exchange window, using the Inboxes and Outboxes off-line, and working with your Personal Address Book, including changing your member information or the way others "see" you.

Starting Electronic Mail

1. To begin, click the E-Mail button in MSN Central.

By using the MSN Indicator icon to select Send Mail, you will always come up in the New Message composition window. Clicking on the main E-Mail button from MSN Central will bring you up in your Inbox, with a display of previously read mail and, in bold face, any mail that you may not have read yet.

2. The Choose Profile appears with MS Exchange Settings highlighted. A profile contains configuration information particular to you as a user and your chosen options for E-Mail and other Exchange services. You will specify where your incoming mail will go, your personal address book, and any other services to which you will be connecting using Exchange. These include not only other on-line services such as America Online and CompuServe, but the Internet as well. It can also include fax drivers and other mail systems. Creating a new Profile is covered later in this chapter. For now, click OK to use the default Profile.

3. If you are just signing on, you may also see a notice pop up announcing you have new mail and asking if it should be opened. If you have mail, by all means, open it! If not you will have your Inbox on your screen, looking very similar to the one in Figure 4.1.

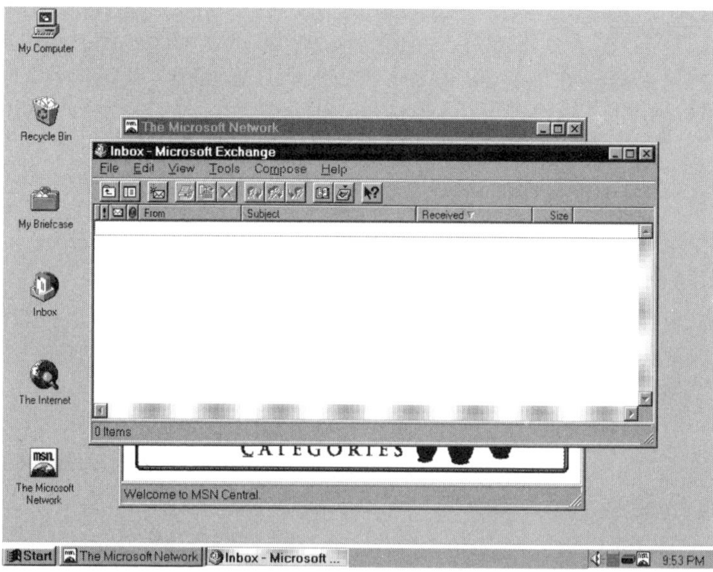

Figure 4.1 *The Microsoft Exchange Inbox is where you receive and read mail.*

Composing and Sending Mail

Composing mail in Microsoft Exchange can be as easy or as complicated as you like. Easy because it is such a simple process, complicated only because there are so many options you can take advantage of.

1. From your Inbox or any Exchange folder, select New Message from the Compose menu.
2. In the To: box, enter the name of an MSN subscriber or an Internet address for users on the Internet or other

services (Internet addresses look like *someuser@somewhere.com*).

If you are unsure of an MSN address, click the To: button, which will bring up the Exchange Address Book. If it is an MSN member address, make sure that the Show Names from the: scroll box reads The Microsoft Network. Enter the address as you think it is, and MSN will find the nearest match. Highlight the name, and the name/address will move from the Name List window to the Message Recipient window. Click OK, and the correct address is filled in the To: box.

---

3. Using the Tab key, move to and fill in the cc: (carbon copy) box if necessary. Always separate multiple names with a semicolon.
4. Tab down to Subject and fill it in. What you enter is what appears in the Description column in the list of mail that comes up in the recipient's Inbox.
5. Click in or Tab to the message area and type your message. Figure 4.2 is a simple E-Mail message, with no cc: filled in.
6. From the File menu, select Send. The bottom left of the window will have a Sending Mail "percent-done" gauge, indicating when the task is complete.

That's all there is to composing and sending simple, fast E-Mail. Of course, you probably want to jazz it up a bit, use some special formatting and include a shortcut and a file or two. We'll be covering all that after we review some of the new icons underneath the menu bar in the Compose window.

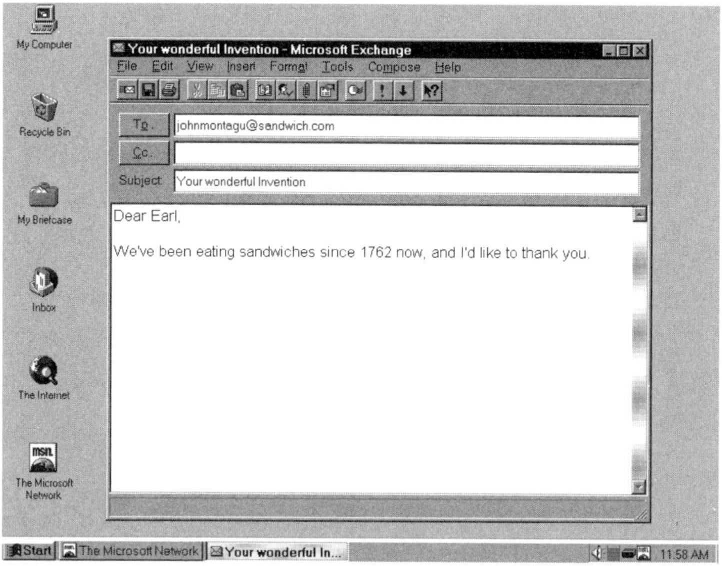

Figure 4.2 *The Compose window where new messages are originated. The task bar has the message's description along with an envelope indicating it is E-Mail.*

The icons are grouped according to task, or tasks related to each other. The first three on the left are send (envelope), save (diskette), and print (printer). Next come the editing icons with the familiar cut (scissors), copy (pieces of paper), and paste (clipboard). Finally are the icons specifically related to sending messages. Let's review these briefly on an individual basis. Most will be covered in much greater detail as we use them.

- **Address book** The book icon refers to the MSN address book. This can be a general one, with all MSN members, or a personal one, where you enter only those names you will be sending mail to on a regular basis. It is here also where you change your member information.

- **Check names** If you are unsure about a name you have entered in the To: box, clicking Check names will check your entry against your personal address book, offering alternate suggestions. It will also give you the option of checking against an alternate list if it cannot find a match, or it may offer different suggestions.
- **Insert file** If you need to insert a file, clicking the paper clip icon will bring up a window from which you can select the file to include. These files can be on the Microsoft Network or on your computer or network.
- **Properties** Each piece of correspondence can have its own properties. The hand holding the letter icon allows you to change these properties from any defaults you have set up.
- **Receipt** Next to the properties icon, all by itself, is the receipt icon. Here is a quick way to ask that a receipt be sent back to you when a message has been read, or to override a previous receipt request.
- **Importance** The next two icons are the "importance" icons. How high is the priority of your letter? Very high (!) or low (↓). How many people out there do you think mark their correspondence with a low importance rating? Perhaps this should be called the "self-esteem" icon.
- **Help** And last, the help icon (↖**?**). When you need help on a particular item, you can always click the help button and drag the **?** to the appropriate spot.

Formatting Text in Exchange

After a short period of time, you'll find that E-Mail becomes more and more a routine part of your day. As you reach that point, you'll find the need to personalize your messages, and have them represent you both in content and the way they look. This is where formatting comes in. To start, we need to add another toolbar.

1. Click the View menu.
2. Select Formatting Toolbar.

Let's take a look at the scroll bars and new icons (Figure 4.3), many of which you will see elsewhere in MSN where formatting messages is an option.

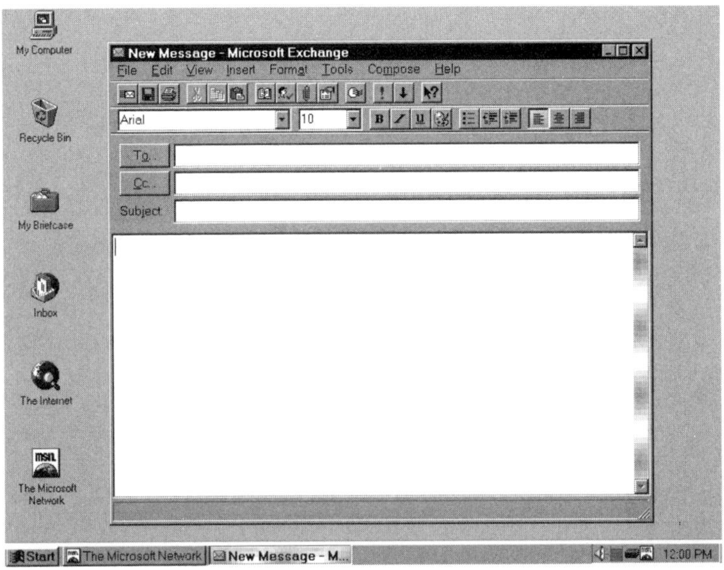

Figure 4.3 *The Compose window with the Formatting toolbar in place. The task bar indicates that this is as yet untitled or not yet described E-Mail message.*

- The scroll bars (with the down arrows to the left) are where one changes the type font's style and size.
- The next group of four govern how the font will look. The first three allow you to choose bold, italic, or underlined. ***Or, you may select all three!*** By clicking the Palette button, you can also change the color.

Like anything else, there are always alternative ways to do things. In this case, if you use the Format menu command, you will not only be able to make all these changes at one time, but will have one additional feature—~~strikeout~~.

The next two groups of three are for simple paragraph formatting.

- The first one is for inserting a bullet (•) before a line.
- The next two in this group are for increasing the left and right indents.
- The last three formatting icons are for paragraph alignment. Shall it be flush left, centered, or flush right? Keep in mind that in this case a paragraph is anything with a carriage return (enter key) following it. This can be 50 words flush left, such as you would think of as a standard paragraph, or a centered, one-line headline.

Don't worry if you can't remember what all the icons do. If you move your mouse slowly over the icons, a "balloon" (or in Microsoft's parlance, a "speedtip") will appear beneath each one, briefly describing its function.

Type another message to experiment on. Highlight the text you wish to change and simply click the correct format icon. Figure 4.4 shows an E-Mail message before it was formatted. Figure 4.5 shows the same message, but with formatting, a shortcut inserted, and an additional file to be sent along with the message.

There is no need to drag the mouse along the entire word or paragraph to select it. To select an entire word, double-click it anywhere; to select a paragraph, triple-click.

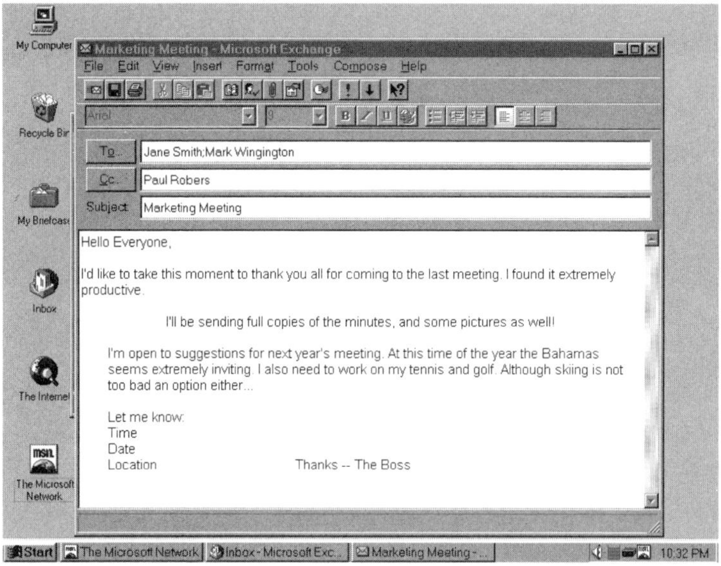

Figure 4.4 *An E-Mail message with only paragraph indents as formatting.*

Figure 4.5 *The same message as Figure 4.4 but with formatting and icons inserted.*

Adding Shortcuts to E-Mail

Shortcuts are a wonderful way to enhance your communications. They are special icons inserted right into the body of your text that will, upon being clicked, automatically take readers exactly where you need them to go. In the Categories area you may have seen a subscription service you thought would be helpful to a colleague at work, or a baseball forum you thought would be interesting to your son or daughter. E-Mail them about it and, instead of telling them where to *look*, include a shortcut to get them right there! After that, of course, they're on their own.

Creating Shortcuts

Of course, to insert a shortcut you must create one in the first place.

1. Go to the area that interests you, such as a forum or specific service.
2. Select its icon by highlighting it.
3. From the File menu, select Create Shortcut.
4. Drag the shortcut icon to the desktop.

Inserting Shortcuts

Now that you've got a shortcut on your desktop, you can insert it into your message.

1. On the desktop, right-click the shortcut icon.
2. Select Copy.
3. In the message area of your E-Mail, right-click to bring up a menu and then click Paste.

That's it! Remember, though, that although you can create shortcuts to just about anything, from files to programs to services to printers, the recipient of your mail must be able to get to those items! It won't do you or them any good to create a shortcut to a printer if it's in the next state and they're not on the network!

Adding Files to Your Messages

There may be times when it is not necessary to create a shortcut or when sending an entire file will better do the job. For instance, you and a co-worker need to exchange and share the work on a spreadsheet.

1. Create your message in the Compose window.
2. From the Insert menu, select File.
3. When the file window appears (Figure 4.6), navigate as you would any Windows 95 explorer window, moving up and down folders to find the appropriate file.

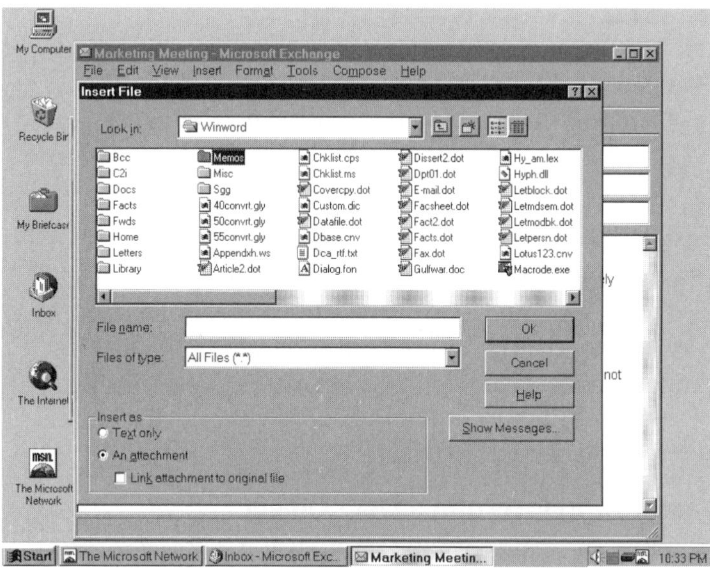

Figure 4.6 *The Insert File window. Treat it as you would any Windows 95 retrieval window.*

4. After selecting the appropriate file, you must decide how you would like to insert it. Text Only will display only the ASCII text on the screen, while sending it as an attachment will send along the actual file, with an

icon representing it in the message. Last, you can link the file *if the recipient has access to the file.* The advantage here is that if the original changes, the link will be updated! To accomplish this, the complete path must be entered, including the *computername**sharename.*

The Show Messages button opens the Insert Message dialog box, from where you can insert messages from other Microsoft Exchange folders.

You can also access the Insert Message dialog box from the Insert menu. Here you will also be presented with the same Text only, Attachment, or Link selections, with a Show Files button to insert files.

5. Click the OK button. You will be returned to the Compose window, with your file icon in place. It is usually helpful to enter some text describing the icon.

Inserting Other Objects into Messages

But why stop at files, shortcuts, and messages? To really liven things up, insert any object to help you make your point. Objects can be anything a program can create—scanned images, video clips, even audio clips. Inserting objects will bring up not only the file you specify, but also the program needed to use it.

Creating and Inserting a New Object

1. From the Compose window, click the Insert menu, then Object.
2. If you are creating a new object and not using an existing file, use the scroll bar to select the file type (Figure 4.7).

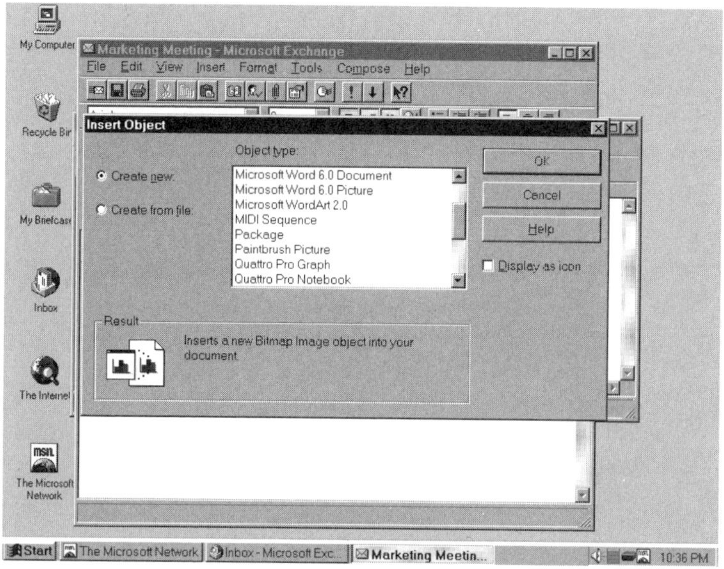

Figure 4.7 *When you Insert a new Object, select from a list the correct software to create the object.*

3. If you want the object represented as an icon, check the Display as Icon box. You will be shown a preselected icon and given the option of changing it. If you do not check the Display as Icon box, the actual object will be part of the message when the message is opened.
4. After selecting the file type, the application necessary to create the file will be opened, overlaid in the Compose window. Figure 4.8 shows the Windows 95 Paint program inserted as part of the Compose window, with a small box, or paint window, of its own. Clicking outside the box when you are finished will return you to the standard Exchange Compose window with the Paint object or icon representing it in place.

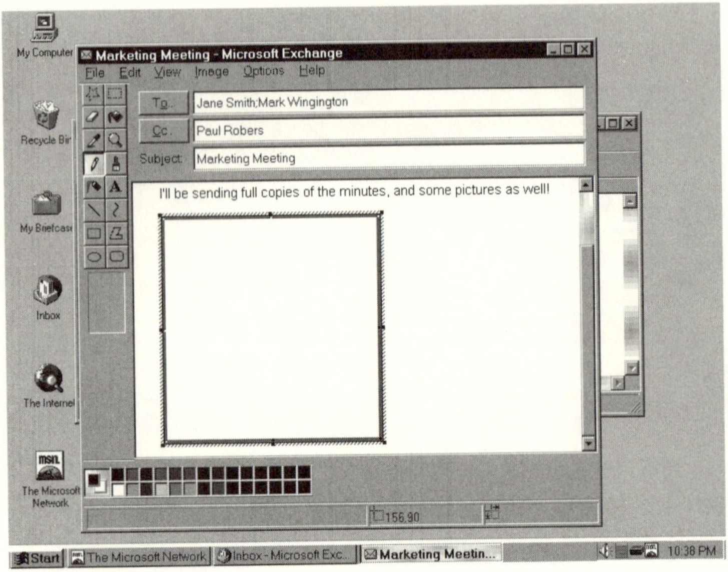

Figure 4.8 *Windows 95 Paint program with the Exchange Compose window.*

Some older programs may not support being used in this manner. You can often tell if a program fully supports this feature, called Object Packaging, by checking the File menu at this point; it will probably contain a Close and Return to Mail menu option.

Inserting an Existing Object

1. From the Compose window, click the Insert menu, then Object.
2. If you are using an existing file, click the Create from File radio button. The Insert Object dialog box in Figure 4.9 pops up. Here you specify the location and name of the file. Exchange will know and activate the program that created it or is necessary to run it. You

can specify that the object itself or an icon representing the object be displayed in the message.

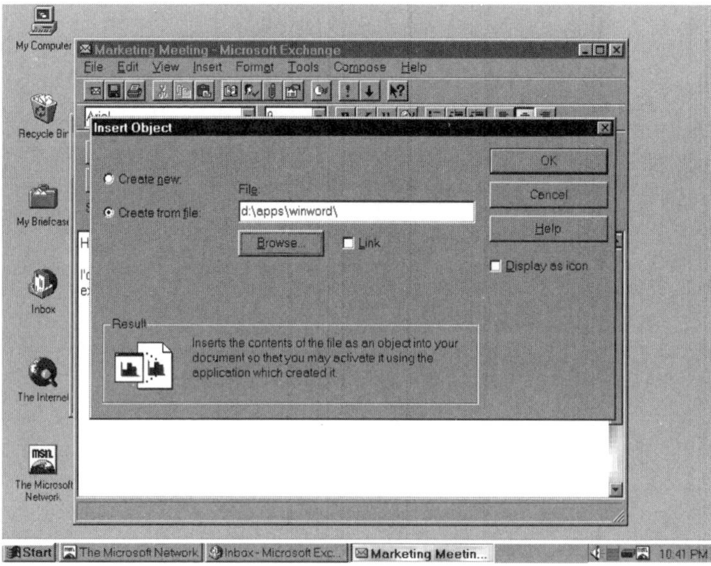

Figure 4.9 *Insert an existing file into an Exchange E-mail message. Enter in the path and file name, or click the Browse button to select from an Insert File window.*

It would seem that with all these options, the file size for your messages would be unlimited (and, for all practical purposes, it usually seems to be). But, alas, that is not the case. Based on the *compressed* size of the image, as compressed by MSN, a file cannot be larger than 2MB. If you are unsure, send it anyway. Although it may say in your Outbox that it is larger than the limit, this message is based on the uncompressed size, and the compressed file may be fine. In any case, if it *is* too large, it will be sent back to you with an explanation.

Creating a Profile

As stated earlier, a Profile is user specific. If you have several people using the same computer, they all should have their own Profile, specifying where their mail should be delivered and saved, their own personal address book, and which information services are available to them. In addition to the default Exchange folders, an unlimited number of personal folders can be created. Mail, incoming faxes, files, and personal documents all come through Exchange, and so each user needs a personal Profile.

1. From MSN Central click the E-Mail button.
2. When the Choose Profile dialog box appears (Figure 4.10), click the New. . . button, which will start the Inbox Setup Wizard.

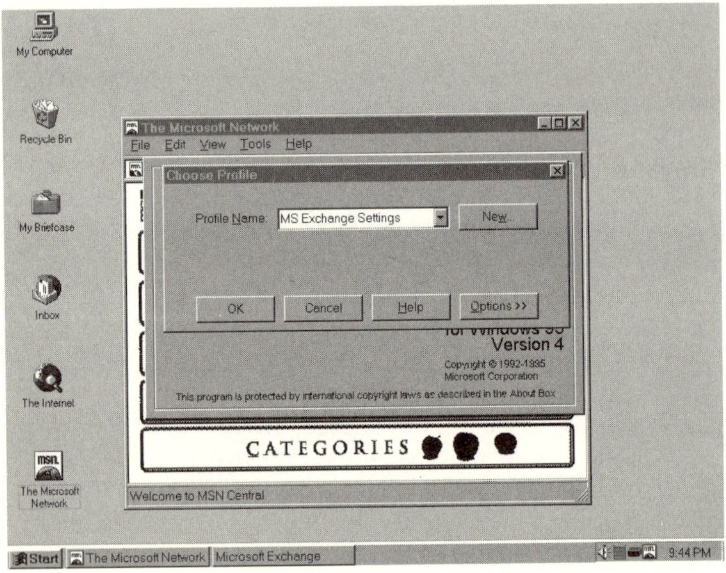

Figure 4.10 *The Choose Profile dialog box. Click the down arrow to select one, or click New to create a new Profile.*

3. The next step in the Setup Wizard is to choose a service. Check the one or ones you need, in this case The Microsoft Network Online Service. Click Next to continue.
4. You must next choose a name for the Profile. Pick any name that makes sense to you, such as your name, and that will differentiate it from other users who share the computer. Click Next to continue.
5. Click Next again to get past the brief description of MSN.
6. The next screen asks you for the name you would like for your personal address book. Change the path and the file name if you wish, but leave the extension (the three letters after the period) alone. Click Next.
7. Now you need to provide the name you wish to use for your personal folders. The same rules apply as above. Make the changes and click Next.
8. Next the Wizard wants to know if when starting up Windows 95 you want your Inbox opened as well. This is personal preference. I don't check my mail immediately each time I sign on to Windows 95, nor do I rush to send new messages but rather do so at different times of the day. You may do otherwise, however. If so, click the proper radio button and then Next.
9. Done! Confirm that what you see is correct, and click Finish (Figure 4.11).

Profiles can be easily modified. From the Start button, select Settings, Control Panel, and then Mail and Fax. When the Profile dialog box appears, click the Show Profiles button to get a list of all the Profiles on your computer.

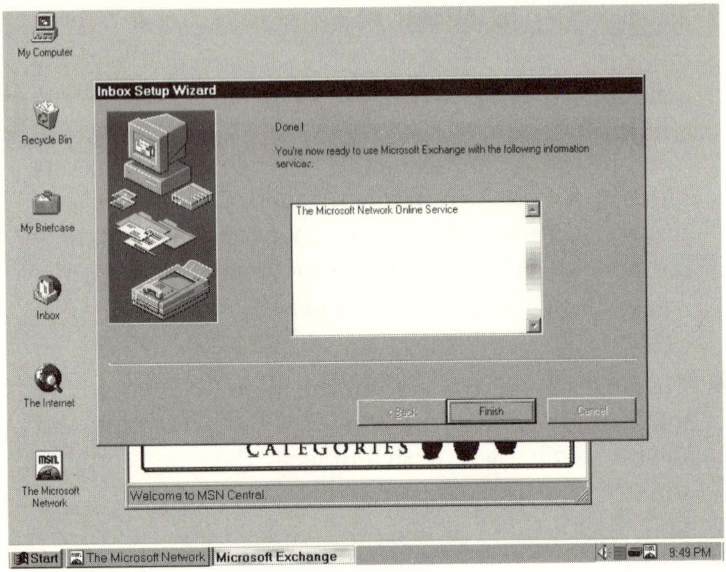

Figure 4.11 *The Inbox Setup Wizard asks you to approve what has been done and click Finish to move on.*

When you are finished, you will see your Inbox, and, sure enough, there is new mail waiting! **Welcome!** appears in bold type, indicating an unread message.

When you first sign on, MSN will notify you if you have mail waiting. If, when you look at your Inbox it is empty, it may be that you have mail on the server that because of various reasons (the server may have been down, or there were other system problems) could not be delivered. To download these new messages to your Inbox, click on the Tools menu and select Deliver Mail Now.

Similarly, if you receive new mail during an on-line session you will not be immediately notified. To see if you have any new mail, open Exchange and click Deliver Mail Now on the Tools menu.

Reading and Responding to Mail

If you have just set up a Profile, you will already have the Inbox on your screen (Figure 4.12). If not, click E-Mail at MSN Central.

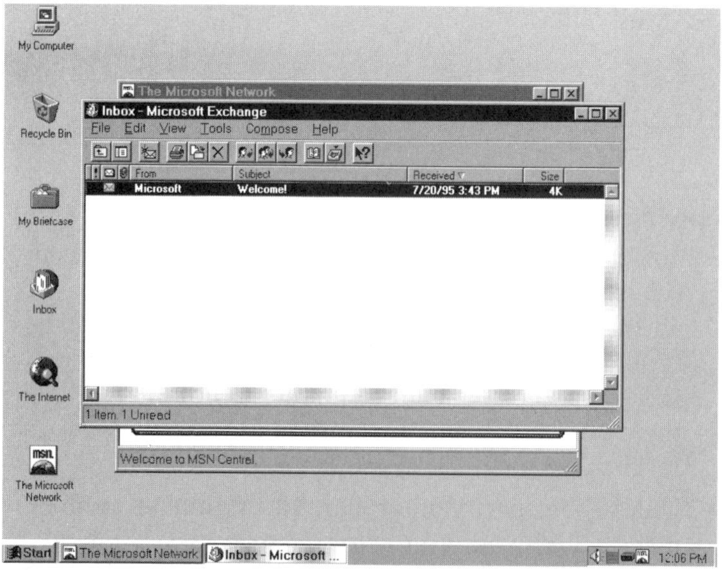

Figure 4.12 *The Inbox immediately after setting up a new Profile. There will be a new Welcome! message, welcoming you to Microsoft Exchange.*

Your E-Mail Address

Reading and responding to mail is pretty straightforward. Of course, in order to receive mail, you have to be able to tell others your address! For users of other on-line services and the Internet, your address will be *memberid*@msn.com (Example: jbsmith@msn.com). This address is *not* case sensitive, so either uppercase or lowercase letters can be used.

Reading Mail

- To open your mail, simply double-click the message you wish to read in your Inbox, and it will open automatically.

Mail that the sender has designated a high priority will have an exclamation point (**!**) to the left, while a low priority will have a down arrow (🡇).

Replying to Mail

- To reply to a message, click the Compose menu, then select Reply to Sender. Your mail will be properly addressed with no further action on your part. After typing your reply and including any attachments or shortcuts, click the File menu, then Send. That's all there is to it! You will be returned to your Inbox, ready for the next task.
- Unless you specify otherwise, the original text will be included with your reply for reference (see below to change this, under Customizing your Folders and Using Icons). For emphasis, you can change the format of the original text, by highlighting it and selecting Font from the Format menu. Of course, you can also change the format by highlighting it and using the individual format icons.

To save an attachment you have received, click the icon representing it to highlight it. From the File menu select Save As and select the appropriate folder. Then, save it with its existing name or change it to one of your choosing.

- You may also automatically send a reply to all of the original recipients. From the Compose menu, select Reply to All.

Mail that has been delivered using the standard mail retrieval methods will be deleted from the server and transferred to your computer. By using Remote Mail to retrieve the message (see Chapter 5) and marking it for Copy, you can leave a copy on the server for a limited time, currently approximately two weeks. The message can then be retrieved again from a different computer or location.

Many of the areas covered in this chapter will come in handy when you are using other services such as bulletin boards. Use the formatting methods described and insert files, objects, and shortcuts. As all this becomes second nature, you will find yourself with more mail than you could handle if you were relying on the post office. The other half of using E-Mail is mail management, which is covered in Chapter 5.

CHAPTER **5**

Custom Mail Management with Exchange

Because E-Mail changes the fundamental ways people communicate on a daily basis, you will find you have more written communications than you ever had before. You don't want to get to the point where you throw up your hands in the face of it all!

From configuring the way your Inbox looks to personalizing your address book, Exchange offers a wide variety of tools to help manage the situation.

Personal Folders

When you first opened your Inbox you probably noticed some more new icons. If the icon bar is not visible, from the View menu select Toolbar.

- **Folders Icon** This icon, second from the left (named the Show/Hide Folder List), will bring a list of all your personal folders in and out of view. Figure 5.1 shows the Inbox, with a selectable view of all available Exchange folders in the left window. Each folder can be customized, and you can add additional folders at any time.

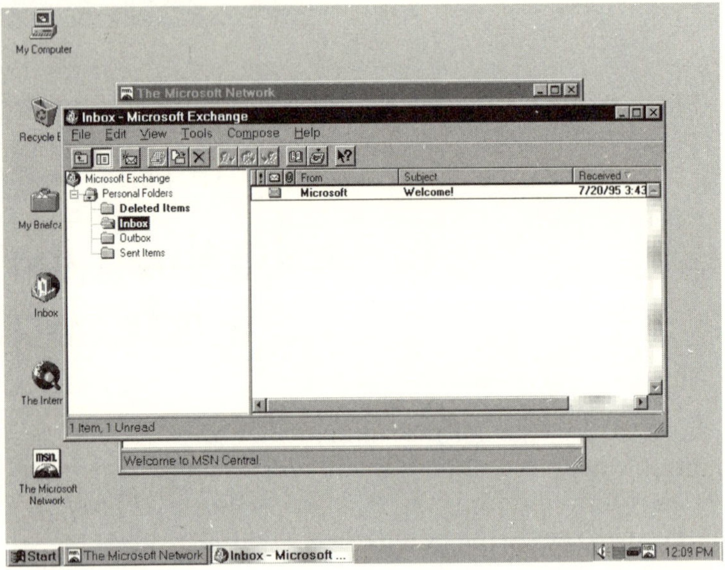

Figure 5.1 *Your Personal Folders can be brought in and out of view for easy navigation.*

Microsoft Exchange sets up a separate collection of folders for each Profile. The main folder is named Personal Folders. Beneath it are four individual folders:

- **Inbox** Here is the destination for incoming mail.
- **Outbox** This temporarily holds messages that you send until they are actually delivered. System problems may delay message transmittal; messages composed off-line (which we'll get to shortly) will also reside here until your next on-line session.
- **Sent Items** This folder holds copies of any messages that you have sent.

- **Deleted Items** This holds any messages that you have marked for deletion but have not yet actually deleted.

The right side of the window shows the content of the open folder. Double-click on any personal folder on the left, and the content list on the right changes.

Adding Personal Folders

You are not limited to the four folders that have been presented here. As with any filing system, additional folders can be used as an aid to organization.

1. Click on the folder into which you wish to place a new folder, highlighting it.
2. On the File menu, select New Folder.
3. Type a name for the folder.
4. Click OK. Your new folder immediately appears on your folder list.

Renaming Folders

1. Highlight the folder you wish to change.
2. Select Rename from the File menu.
3. Type in the new name.

Deleting Folders

1. Click on the folder you need to delete.
2. From the File menu select Delete, and the deed is done.

Moving and Copying Items Between Folders

When organizing your files you may find that you become more particular about where your mail, faxes, and other MSN items are being stored. Moving files from one folder to another is just a few clicks of the mouse.

1. Make sure that the message or other item to be moved is closed.
2. From the File menu select either Move or Copy.

3. When the Move or Copy window pops up, click the folder that will receive the file, then OK, and the file will be copied or moved.

You can also move an item with Drag and Drop. Highlight the closed item to be moved and drag it to the desired folder.

Move and copy icons can also be made available on the toolbar. See the sections that follow Using the Exchange Icon Toolbar and Customizing the Exchange Icon Toolbar.

Adding, Changing and Removing Columns

The column presentation within your folders is not set in stone: neither the number of columns you see nor the column headings. Columns can be added, deleted, replaced, and resized.

1. From the View menu select Columns.
2. When the Columns dialog box pops up (Figure 5.2), highlight the column title you would like to add to your folder from those listed in the Available columns box, then click Add. At last count there were more than 30 possible choices!
3. The column heading will move to the right window, Show the Following Columns.
4. In the Width box adjust the size of a column. Depending on the characteristics of the column contents, this adjustment will be in number of characters across or in the number of pixels (dots on the screen.)

Column widths can also be changed directly in a folder. Simply click the header bar between the columns you wish to change and drag the column to the desired width.

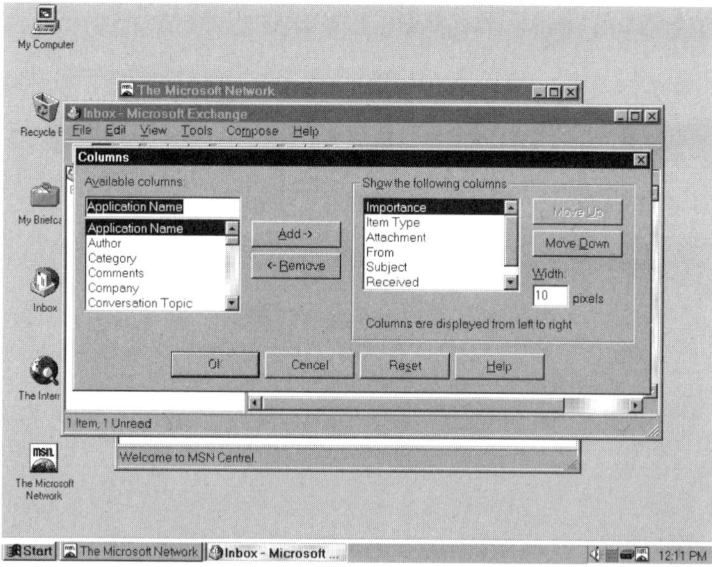

Figure 5.2 *Different folders can have different configurations. Select the column heading that makes the most sense to you.*

5. Select where you want the column headings to appear in relation to each other. Highlight a heading and click the Move Up or Move Down buttons until you are satisfied with the order of your columns.
6. To remove a column, highlight its heading in the Show the Following Columns box, and click Remove.

Sorting Items in Your Personal Folders

Items in your folders can be sorted in any order by column heading, either ascending or descending. Each individual folder can have a different sort order.

1. With the folder you need to sort open, click on the View menu.
2. Select Sort.

3. Click on the down arrow to get a list of available sort options. These will include, but not necessarily be limited to, the column headings in the open folder.
4. Click the Ascending or Descending radio button.
5. Click OK.

You can quickly sort all the messages in a given column by double-clicking on the column title. For example, to see all the message from a given correspondent, double-click on From and scroll down through the messages—they'll all be grouped by sender. The default setting for this is to group them by time and date received.

Using the Exchange Icon Toolbar

Most of the icons on the Exchange Toolbar will be familiar, but some are unique to Exchange.

- **New Message** After the Up One Level and Show/Hide Folder List icons on the left is the New Message icon (envelope). This brings the same result as selecting New Message from the Compose menu.
- **Move** Moving past the printer icon we find the Move Item icon. This will bring up the Move dialog box, prompting you to select a folder to which to move a highlighted file.
- **Delete** This icon will send a highlighted item to the Deleted Items folder.

Don't worry if you mistakenly delete an item! It's not *really* gone for good, at least not yet. Mail is only permanently deleted when you use the delete icon from within the Deleted Items folder.

The next group of three icons all deal with replying to mail. They are the equivalent of the reply options you find on the Compose menu.

- **Reply to Sender** Automatically addresses your reply to the person who sent you the mail in the first place.
- **Reply to All** Automatically replies to everyone on the distribution list of the original message.
- **Forward** The last of the group of three. Forward sends the original message, with any additions you make, on to another recipient entirely.
- **Address Book** The icon with a picture of an open book to the right of the reply icons opens the MSN Address Book. We'll discuss the Address Book at length shortly.
- **Inbox** Clicking this will always bring you back to your Inbox, for easy mail retrieval.

Customizing the Exchange Icon Toolbar

The icons so far discussed are the defaults selected by Microsoft, but you are by no means stuck with these choices! If you find yourself using commands frequently and wishing they were available to you as an icon, your wishes can come true. Almost every command accessed from the pull-down menus can be added to the Exchange Toolbar.

1. From the Tools menu select Customize Toolbar.
2. When the dialog box in Figure 5.3 appears, highlight the icons you wish to add in the Available buttons window.
3. Click Add to move them to the toolbar buttons window.
4. To remove a button, highlight it in the Toolbar buttons window, and click Remove.
5. When you are finished making your selections, click OK.

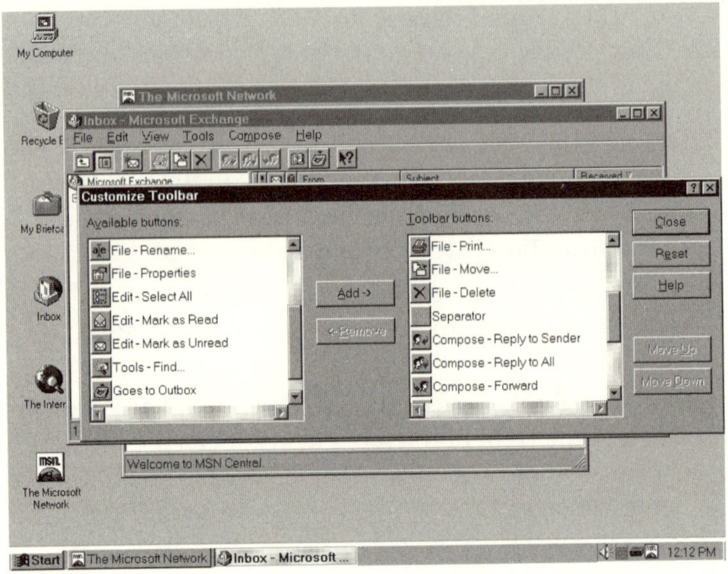

Figure 5.3 *Customize the toolbar so it has icons of the commands you use most frequently.*

6. To return to the defaults, click Reset in the Customize Toolbar box.

Using the Microsoft Exchange Address Book

The Microsoft Exchange Address Book is much more than a simple address book. It can become your complete database, both professional and personal, for all the people with whom you communicate on-line or via fax.

Figure 5.4 shows the basic Address Book dialog box. It is the first thing you see when looking up a name to fill in the To: box when addressing mail, when looking up a MSN member's address, when creating a distribution list, or when updating your personal Address Book. When you access the Address Book from your Inbox or other Personal Folders, it will look like the one in Figure 5.5.

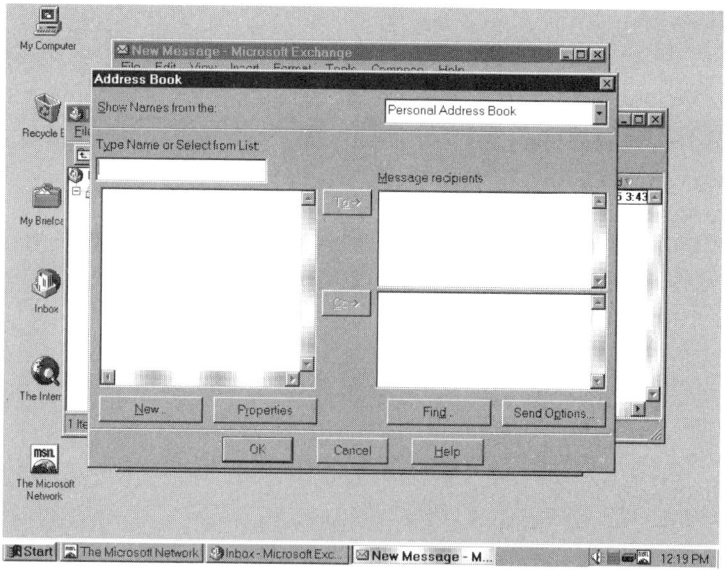

Figure 5.4 *The Microsoft Exchange Address Book as it looks when it is accessed from the Compose window.*

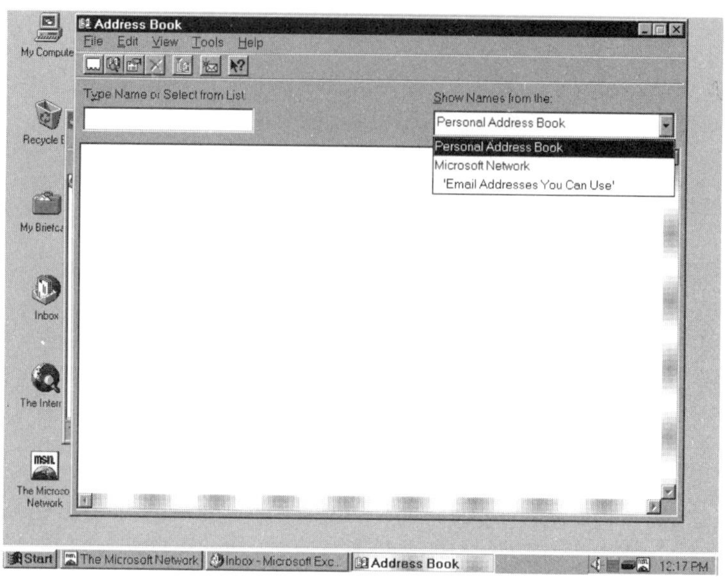

Figure 5.5 *Another view of the Address Book. This time it was accessed from a personal folder.*

You must first tell Exchange which database, or Address Book, you will be using. The Show Names from the: scroll box lists the choices you have, in this case, Personal Address Book and The Microsoft Network.

As you meet people on-line with whom you think you may have further communication, you can easily add them to your Personal Address Book. It is much quicker to look them up there than going through all the MSN members, which is what using The Microsoft Network Address Book does. And, since your personal Address Book is kept on your hard disk, you can prepare any off-line or remote mail (discussed later) more readily. If you find your Address Book getting cluttered with people you rarely send mail to, it is also easy to remove them.

Adding Names to Your Personal Address Book from the MSN Member List

1. You can get to the Address Book from any folder by clicking the address book icon.
2. If you are on-line, the Show Names from the: scroll box may read Personal Address Book or the Microsoft Network. Make sure it is the Microsoft Network, as this is where we will find our first name to add.
3. In the Type Name or Select from List entry box, type the name to be added to your personal Address Book.
4. When the correct name or E-Mail address appears in the left hand window, select it by highlighting, then click the Properties button.

If you cannot find the name you are looking for and you are *sure* it is in there somewhere, use the Find button. Click find and then type any contiguous string of letters in the name you are searching for.

5. The dialog box in Figure 5.6 will appear, giving you (perhaps) a wealth of information. I say perhaps because there will only be what the MSN member chose to enter! This information cannot be changed by anyone but the member listed.

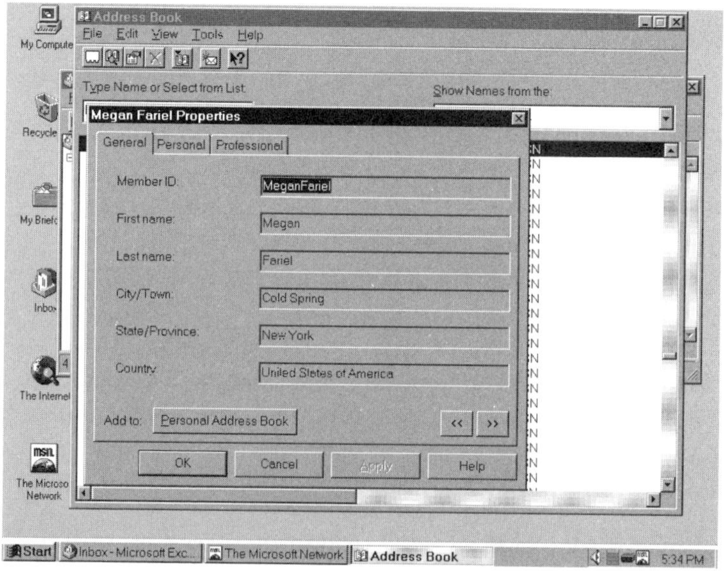

Figure 5.6 *A Member Properties dialog box. The information cannot be changed by anyone but the member.*

6. Notice the tabs at the top of the Member Properties form. Take some time to flip through them. The right and left arrows at the bottom right will page from next or previous members.
7. Click Add To Personal Address Book, and then OK to return to the previous screen.
8. The new entry will now appear in your Personal Address Book list.

There are two quick ways to add a new address to your Personal Address book when you have received mail. After the mail is opened, right-click the name in the From: field, and then click Add to Personal Address Book on the pop-up menu. Or, by double-clicking the name with the left mouse button, the Member Properties box appears. From here you can click the Add to: Personal Address Book.

Adding Names to Your Personal Address Book from Other Services

There will come a time when you need to add names to your Personal Address Book without looking them up in the Properties box or the MSN membership list. It may be a stack of business cards you have collected, all with E-Mail addresses from places ranging from CompuServe to the Internet. You will also find that more and more people you already communicate with in a more traditional fashion are going on-line.

1. Open E-Mail.
2. Click the Address Book icon from any folder or the Compose window.
3. If you selected Address Book from the Compose window, click the New... button with Personal Address Book as the selected names list.
4. If you selected Address Book from your personal folders, click the New Entry icon, which looks like a Rolodex card.
5. When the New Entry screen appears (Figure 5.7), highlight the entry type. Depending on which selection you make, you will get a slightly different data entry screen.

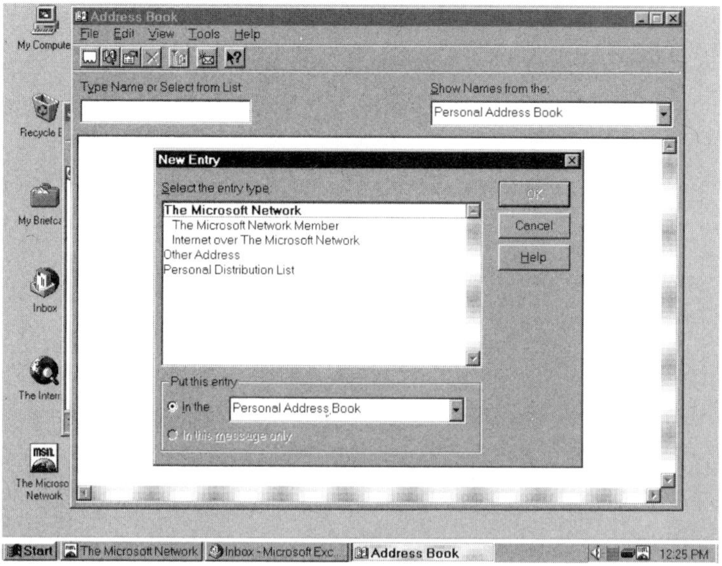

Figure 5.7 *The Personal Address New Entry screen. When adding a new entry to your Personal Address Book, the first thing you must tell MSN is what type of service the new entry is using.*

6. Figure 5.8 shows a generic type, which pops up when Other Address is highlighted. Enter the Display Name exactly as you would like it to appear in your Personal Address Book.
7. Enter the E-Mail address. A CompuServe address would be entered as, for example, 75689.7866. Notice that the comma in a traditional CompuServe address has to be replaced with a period.
8. In the E-Mail Type box, enter the service, in this case CompuServe.

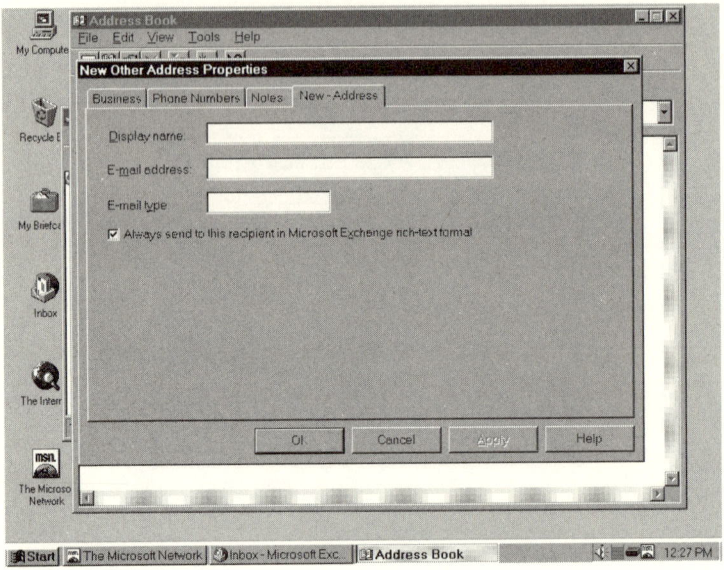

Figure 5.8 *The generic New Entry dialog box. This pops up when Other Address is highlighted in the Personal Address New Entry screen.*

9. If you are sending mail to another user of a messaging system that can display formatted text, check off the Always send to this recipient in Microsoft Exchange Rich Text Format (RTF). If the box is not checked, the messages will be sent in plain text only.
10. Click OK to return to the original Address Book window.

If you do not know, and simply cannot find an address you are looking for, you can send mail to postmaster@<domain>, where domain is the service they are on. In this case it would be postmaster@MSN.com, but could just as easily be postmaster@compuserve.com.

The postmaster will forward the mail, and the person has the option of reading and responding, or not.

Creating a Personal Distribution List

There will be many occasions when you will need to send the same messages to a group of different people. Perhaps you have scheduled a meeting where you expect a specific committee to attend and need to constantly update each member. Or perhaps you have a group of friends to invite to a party! You can have multiple distribution lists to accommodate many different situations.

1. Open Exchange and, from either your personal folders or the Compose window, open the Address Book.
2. Make sure that the Show Names From: box reads Personal Address Book.
3. From the File menu select New Entry (or click the New button or the New Entry/Rolodex card icon).
4. When the New Entry window appears, highlight Personal Distribution List and click OK.
5. The New Personal Distribution List Properties window appears. Enter the name of the list as you would like it to appear in your Personal Address Book.
6. Click the Add/Remove Members button.
7. Select the names to include in the list. These can be from your Personal Address Book list or from the Microsoft Network member list. Highlight the names and click Members to move the names from the left window to the Personal Distribution List window.
8. If the name is not in either list, you will have to enter it as a New Entry. Click the New... button and then select the entry type. Be careful not to select Personal Distribution List, as you will wind up in an endless loop, having been returned to the New Personal Distribution List Properties window! For more information on adding new entries, see the earlier section

Adding New Names to Your Personal Address Book from Other Services.

9. When you have finished adding names, click OK.

Updating Your Member Information

Your own member information may appear in many spots on the Microsoft Network. This is not the confidential information such as credit card numbers or other banking data that you provided when you signed up, but rather more personal points. When you post a message to a bulletin board, or when you E-Mail someone, the person reading the message has the option of "seeing" who you are. Of course, you determine just what they see.

This is more than an area for E-Mail addresses. You can include personal and business phone numbers, addresses, hobbies and other special interests, even marital status!

1. Open E-Mail by clicking the E-Mail button in MSN Central.
2. When your Inbox appears, click the Address Book icon.
3. Make sure the Show Names from: scroll box reads The Microsoft Network. Enter your name and, when it appears in the list below, highlight it.
4. Click on Properties from the File menu, or click the Properties icon.
5. When the dialog box in Figure 5.9 appears, tab through it entering the appropriate information. All the fields do not have to be filled in.
6. Click OK when finished. This will save your information on MSN.

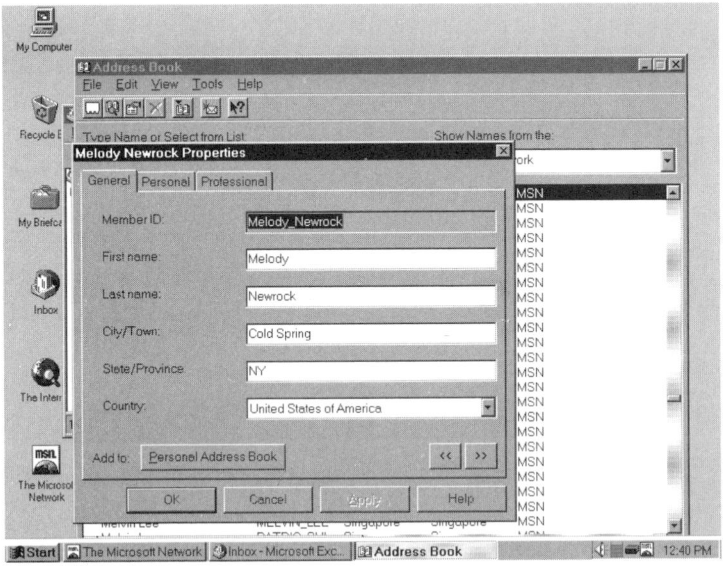

Figure 5.9 *Updating your own member properties. Notice that all the fields but Member ID have a white background indicating that you can change the information.*

Addressing Internet Mail

Because the Internet is such a vast network, literally linking thousands of computers around the world, addressing the mail can seem confusing. The screen in Figure 5.10 shows the New Entry screen for adding an Internet address to your Personal Address Book, but what to do may not seem so clear if you are entering an address given to you on a business card or over the phone.

For example, if I were at the Bosh Kosh University, tied into their network, I might have an address that looked like this: melodynewrock@bku.edu. In the New Internet over The Microsoft Network Properties box shown in Figure 5.10, the E-Mail address would be melodynewrock, the domain name is bku.edu, and finally my name as it would appear in your personal address book, Melody Newrock!

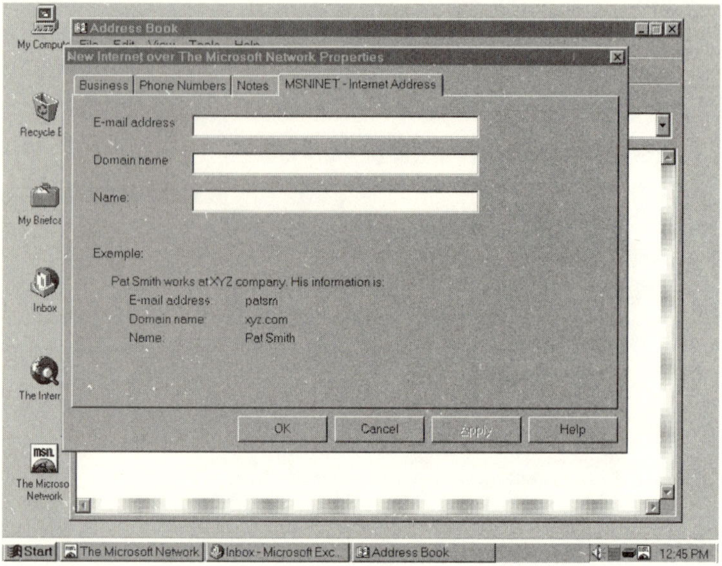

Figure 5.10 *Adding an Internet address to your Personal Address Book.*

If you are having trouble sending mail to an Internet or any other address, notify the Postmaster. Send a message to "Postmaster" on MSN describing the exact problem you are having, including the address to which you are trying to send the mail. You will get a prompt reply containing a solution.

Using Exchange Off-line

Depending on your communications needs, composing and reading mail can be time consuming. Microsoft Exchange gives you the capability of composing new messages off-line for later transmittal. You also have the ability to go on-line to retrieve messages to be read later while off-line.

Composing while Off-line

1. Start Exchange by double-clicking the inbox icon on your desktop.
2. From the Compose menu select New Message.
3. Compose your new message, using all the techniques described in Composing and Sending Mail, above. Because you are off-line, mail should be addressed to those in your Personal Address Book.
4. Click the send (envelope) icon, or from the File menu select Send.
5. After "Sending" the mail, it is moved to your Outbox, waiting until you sign on again. In this way you can compose and accumulate multiple messages while off-line, sending them all off at once!
6. When you have finished all your letters, from the Tools menu select Deliver Now.
7. The Sign-In screen will appear. Enter your password and click Connect.
8. As you are being connected to send your outgoing mail, MSN will check for new messages to be sent to your Inbox.
9. If you switch to your Outbox you will see each of the items you just completed move out of the window as they are delivered.
10. Check your Sent Items folders. Each Piece of E-Mail that was just delivered should be listed.

If during the session you have received new mail, a New Mail indicator will be visible on the task bar.

Retrieving Mail for Remote Use

The more you come to depend on E-Mail for standard correspondence, the more mail you will receive. You will find that using it to communicate with business people instead of using the more traditional mail and fax will often bring a more timely response. And let's not forget that in addition to communicating through bulletin boards and chat sessions, sending mail to other MSN members you've met on-line can become a fairly automatic response. In a short time your Personal Address Book will grow and grow while amount of incoming mail may appear unmanageable. Reading this on-line can be cumbersome as well as costly in connect time.

Don't worry. MSN and Exchange offer several mail management tools. They allow you to quickly log on to MSN and have only those messages you wish to read sent to your computer. Each can be individually marked to be downloaded, to be copied and then downloaded (leaving a copy on the MSN server for later retrieval from another computer or site), or simply deleted. Your choices can even be made automatically! Use the Exchange filter to select by date and time, by subject matter, or even by author. So you see, that deluge of mail will not really be so overwhelming.

1. Double click the inbox icon on your desktop to open Exchange.
2. From the Tools menu select Remote Mail.
3. In the Remote Mail window, select Filter from the Tools menu.
4. Figure 5.11 shows the Filter dialog box. Use this to pre-select only those messages you are looking for. You can specify only messages from a certain author, on a specific subject matter, those that were sent directly to you, or only those copied (cc) to you.

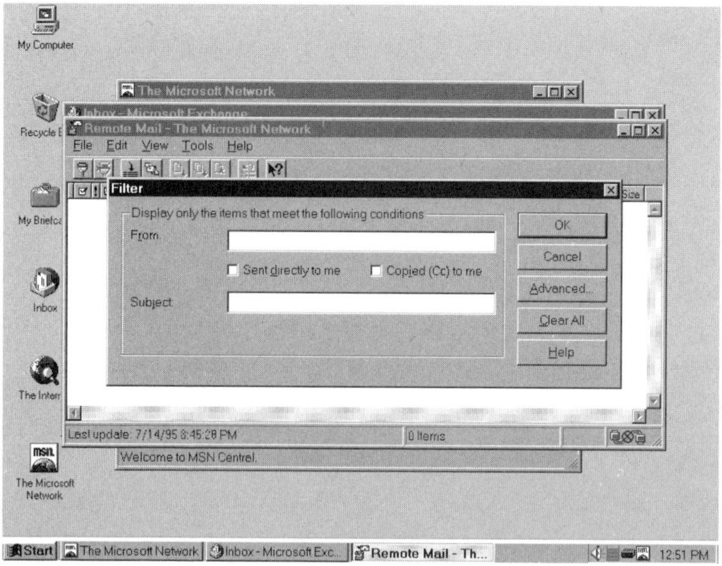

Figure 5.11 *The Remote Mail Filter dialog box. Use this so only those messages that you are looking for are downloaded to your computer to be read at a later time.*

5. If you get a *lot* of mail, you do not have to go through each header. You can further filter them out. Figure 5.12 is the Advanced Filter options dialog box, which appears when you click the Advanced... button on the box in Figure 5.11. Options include Size of file (least and most), Date Received (From and To), Importance and Sensitivity levels, Only Unread Items, and Items with Attachments. In fact, you can make a negative filter by specifying all the information, and checking off Only items that do *not* match these conditions. Click OK to return to the previous dialog box and then OK to return to Remote Mail.
6. From Remote mail select the Tools menu and then Connect and Update Headers.

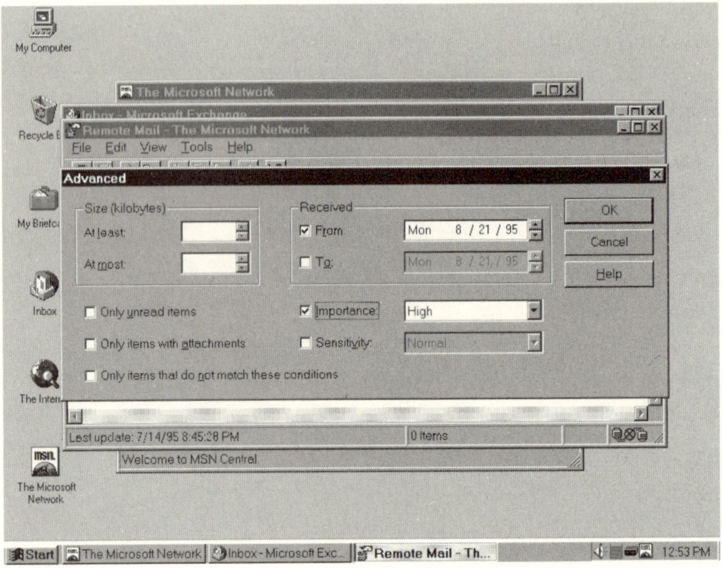

Figure 5.12 *The Advanced Remote Mail Filter dialog box can further filter out unwanted mail.*

7. When the MSN Sign-In screen appears, enter your password and click Connect.
8. As MSN checks for new mail, it will check your Outbox for any mail to be delivered.
9. Your new mail will be listed in the Remote Mail window. Highlight each item you are interested in and from the Edit menu select Mark to Retrieve, Mark to Copy, or Mark to Delete.
10. Select Transfer Mail from the Tools menu. You will be apprised of file size, transfer time, and the number of files to be sent. Click Continue to have the mail sent.
11. Return to your Inbox and open and read your mail at your leisure!

Customizing Mail and Remote Mail

Microsoft Exchange will work the way that you work. You can set default preferences for everything from the way your mail will look to how it will be sent and what will happen when it is sent. These preferences can always be changed if you find that something different comes more naturally; simply return to Exchange and change your settings.

1. From any Exchange folder or the Compose window, select Options from the Tools menu.
2. Notice the six tabs that appear on top (Figure 5.13). Each of these tabs deals with a different aspect of how mail will be composed, sent, and delivered.

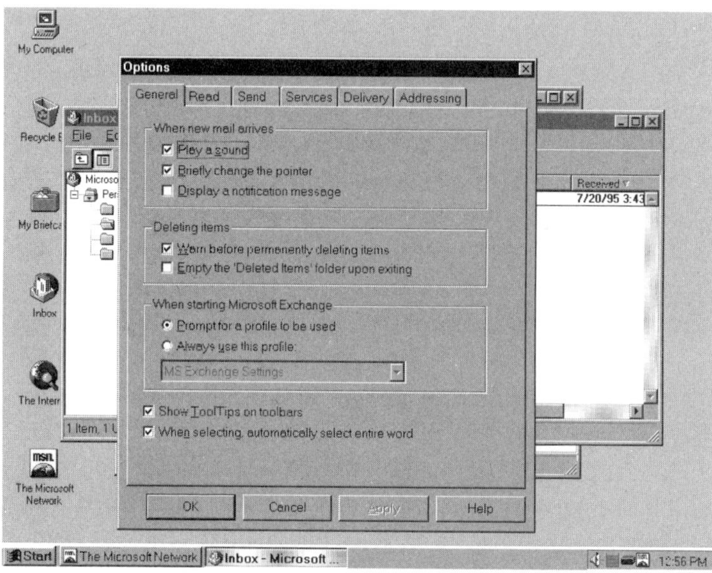

Figure 5.13 *The Microsoft Exchange Options dialog box allows you to customize the way Exchange actually behaves.*

- **General** Here you control new mail notification, deleting items, default Profiles, whether to keep those little hints on toolbar icons, and how words and letters are selected.

- **Read** This tab deals with how Exchange behaves after you have moved or deleted an open item (move to the next item or exit) and how it will handle mail you are responding to (whether to include the original, whether to indent, whether to change the color, and so forth.)
- **Send** Send is where you set the Compose defaults. The defaults control the font used, whether to have Delivered and Read receipts, the Sensitivity and Importance levels, and whether copies will always be sent to your Sent Items folder.
- **Services** Here is the list of the information services available in this Profile. Don't take this too literally! Unlike the more traditional scope of information service, in this case the included services are Personal Address Book, Personal Folders, and The Microsoft Network On-line Service! From here you can add or delete a service by clicking the appropriate button or display the service's properties to make certain changes.

Highlight Personal Address Book and click on Properties. The dialog box in Figure 5.14 appears, allowing you to change the name, the path, and the order in which the list of names is displayed. These options are also available from the Addressing tab.

Highlight The Microsoft Network On-line Service and click on Properties. The dialog box in Figure 5.15 appears. The Transport tab is on top, with check boxes for different connection defaults. The Address Book tab has only one check box. Here is where you tell Exchange to always connect to MSN to verify the names in the To: box. This can slow things down considerably! And you will not be able to compose new messages off-line for later transmittal.

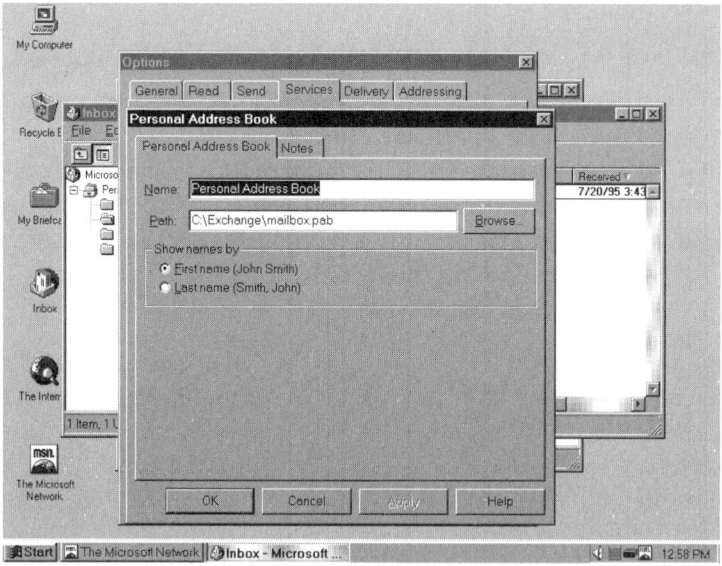

Figure 5.14 *The Services Options dialog box includes options for your Personal Address Book.*

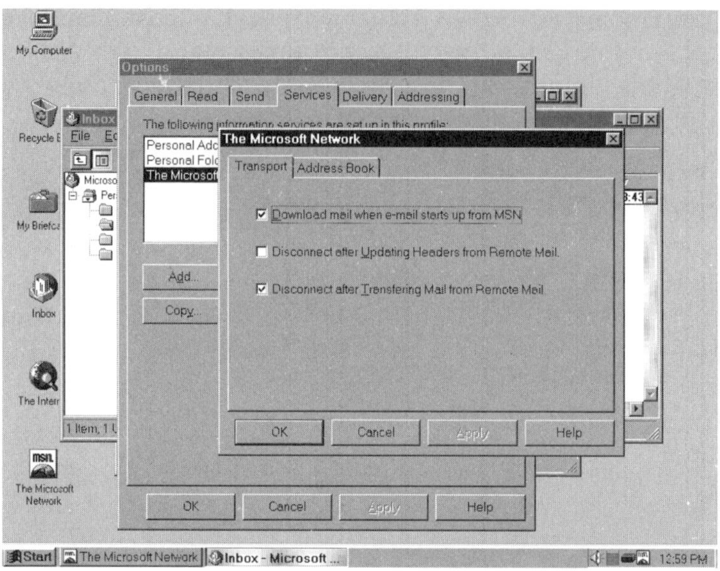

Figure 5.15 *Services' Options give the ability to change how Exchange delivers your mail and to specify whether to disconnect from the Microsoft Network afterwards.*

- **Delivery** You determine in which folder your new mail will go and here is where you do it.

  If you use more than one information service you can specify the order in which Exchange should use for sending messages. In other words, should Exchange first send mail using the Microsoft Network, which is the default, Microsoft Fax, or yet another information service you to which you also subscribe?
- **Addressing** There are three items on the Addressing tab. First, when the Address Book appears, which address list should be presented first: your Personal Address Book, the Microsoft Network address book, or some other one? It is usually your Personal Address Book, but you may select another. Second, you can also select another location for your personal addresses. And last, here is where you tell Exchange the order of the lists it should look at to check addresses.

So you see, Microsoft Exchange and MSN E-Mail are rich in features, enabling you send complex and highly-formatted communications. But despite all their capabilities, they are easy to learn and intuitive to use.

CHAPTER 6

Chatting: Making Friends and Finding People with Shared Interests

Chatting on-line is actually somewhat like an old-fashioned party-line. I say somewhat only because you have more control than you would with a party-line. Here is where you will find others with common interests for real-time conversations. Of course, these conversations are written, not oral. And much like the old teletypes of the past, you type in what you want to say and then wait for someone, or someones, to type a response.

Chat rooms are for people to communicate with others with similar interests and needs. When I recently used the Find tool to display all the chat rooms currently on MSN, there were a greater number of locations found than Find could deliver! They varied in subject from Parenting in the 90's to Theater Chat to Wills, Probates, and Trusts. Almost every area has a chat room, and many have more than one. Some may be subsets of a specific topic, while others may be specially designated as small chats, limited to two, six, eight, or ten people. They are almost always recognizable by their "talk balloon" icons, part of which may be hidden by a more subject-related icon. (See Figure 6.1.)

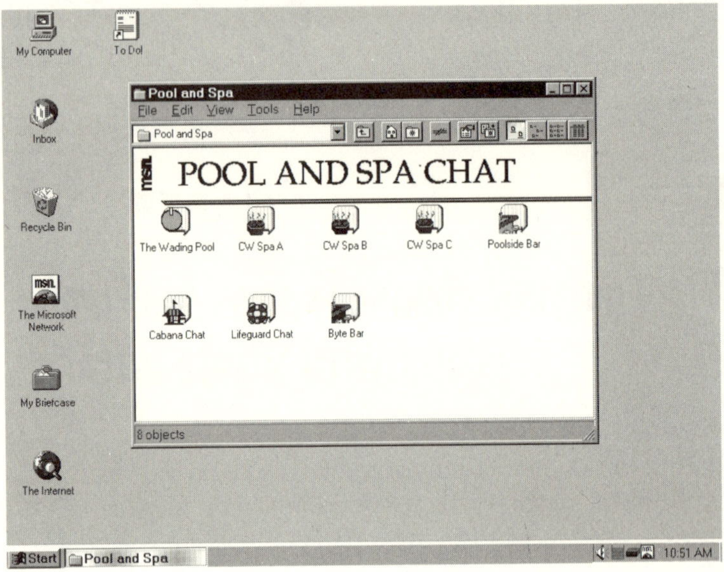

Figure 6.1 *Chat rooms are almost always (but not always) represented by a talk balloon icon. It is often partially obscured by a small graphic depicting the chat subject.*

The idea here is to just jump in. If you are nervous about contributing at first, there is no rush. In fact, in both chat rooms and bulletin boards it may be better to wait to get the feel and tone of the area. Enter a chat room and observe. Remember, all that others can see of you is what *you* have elected to include in your Member Information (from your Personal Address Book). Soon after you may find yourself following one or more conversations rather avidly, with your fingers itching to send a reply, or you may want to initiate your own conversation.

A good way to get started is with the small chat rooms in Chat World (Figure 6.2). There are several, each limited to two, three, four, five, or ten individuals. Have some fun learning the ropes and feel more confident when entering the special interest chat rooms and special event auditoriums.

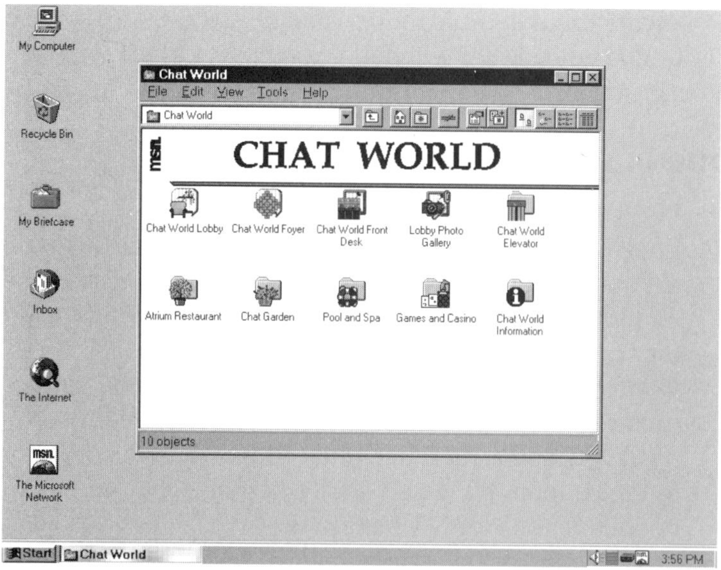

Figure 6.2 *Chat World is a wonderful place to meet new and longtime MSN members.*

1. Contact a friend or colleague who is also on MSN and arrange to meet first at a predetermined time in the Chat World Lobby or the Chat World Foyer. Each of these Chat Rooms are central meeting places which can accommodate up to 50 MSN members at a time. The Lobby is monitored 24 hours a day (and so is a good place for children), while the Foyer is not.

2. From MSN Central, go to Member Assistance, then Member Activities and on to Chat World. After meeting in one of these two, you can then move on to one of the smaller, more private chat rooms. Check out the Spa or go into the Garden. In any one you enter, select one of the chat rooms. Or take the Chat World Elevator. Each floor has rooms limited to a number of people corresponding to the floor number.

Beware though, these rooms cannot be reserved, so try to pick a time when MSN will not be too busy! Or just follow the instructions below to jump right into the main chat areas.

Entering a Chat Room

1. From MSN Central click the Categories button.
2. Look over the various interest groups, such as Business & Financial or Arts & Entertainment. These areas are only the tip of the iceberg. Each one is further and further broken down, until you zero in on just what you want. Double-click on an area that interests you, and then continue clicking, moving down the category tree until you find a chat that you'd like to join. In addition to the balloon, which is usually part of a chat icon, it may have the word "Chat" in the title.
3. For example, by clicking Interest, Leisure & Hobbies, you will see, among others, the Games and Gaming icon. After double-clicking on it, click on the Games and Gaming Forum folder and the Games window appears. Look over the assorted icons (Figure 6.3). There is a Games newsletter, which is updated regularly and various bulletin boards and folder icons, which lead further down to more and more specific areas such as Magic and Video Games. This is how most, if not all of the special interest areas work. Just keep clicking and exploring, and you never know what you may find. When you click on Games Chat, you will enter a chat room.

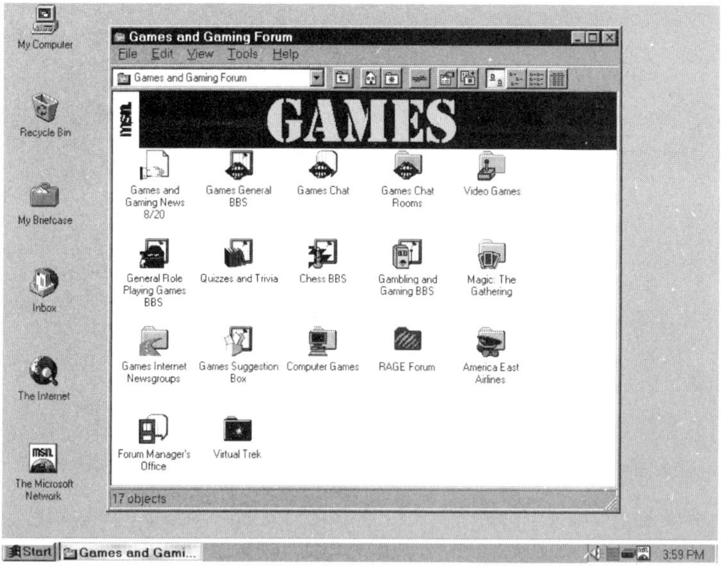

Figure 6.3 *A typical category can have several chat rooms at the first level, or folders with nothing but more chat rooms.*

When you first enter any chat room, you will notice it is broken into three areas, with a Send button on the bottom (Figure 6.4).

MSN Today frequently lists special "meetings" taking place in various "auditoriums." These are really chat rooms with special names. You may be asked to enter one room to ask questions of the "speaker" or send any other message, while the chat is displayed in another. But they still are essentially chat rooms and will all work the same way. The Special Events Category in Figure 6.5 shows the Babbage Auditorium where many guest "speakers" appear. Next to it is a chat room icon titled Ask Questions Here where you ask questions of the "speaker" in the Babbage Auditorium.

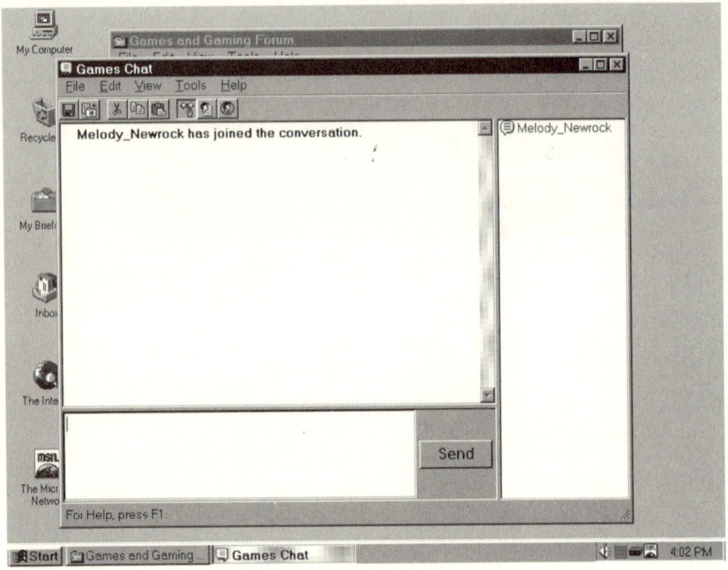

Figure 6.4 *Once inside, chat rooms all look the same, but like live forums each will have a distinct atmosphere.*

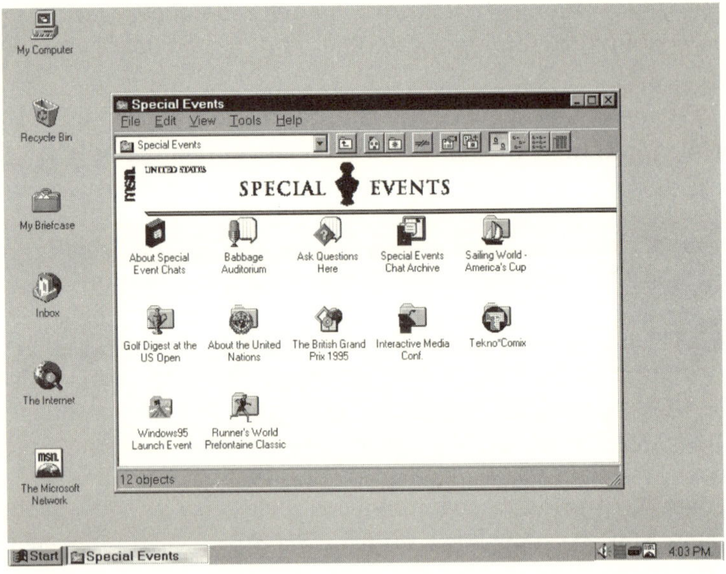

Figure 6.5 *Special events will often have two chat rooms. In one you ask questions which are then screened before being sent on to another by a moderator.*

Chat History Pane

The largest area, in the center and left side of the window, is the Chat History pane. Here is where all participant's messages are displayed until you clear the history. Messages are always added to the bottom, and any that appear in bold type are notifications automatically generated by chat. These include messages indicating who has joined or left the chat.

If they annoy you, these last can be suppressed. Select Options from the Tools menu. Indicate your preferences under Notify Me When by checking off or leaving blank the notification boxes and display preferences.

If you find the chat difficult to follow, changing the line spacing may help. From the Tools menu click Options. Change the Insert Blank Line Between Messages to the setting which is most comfortable to you.

Don't feel that you are limited to the letters on your keyboard. Like any animated conversation, expression is important! There are many expressions available to you from the keyboard, from happy faces, to ones of disapproval. These expressions have evolved over the years and are commonly used and recognized. Take a look at the collection below, some of which must be read sideways.

- Crying :'-)
- Grinning :-[) or :D
- Hugs {},[]
- Kiss X
- Smiling :-)
- Winking ;-)
- Yelling :-[]

Typing in ALL UPPER CASE also represents yelling. Try to avoid it, as it is not considered acceptable behavior.

Because you will be typing on the fly, trying to get your words out as quickly as you speak, try using some of the gestures listed below. These too have developed over time and are recognized by many in the on-line world:

- BTW — By the way
- IMHO — In my humble opinion
- IOW — In other words
- LOL — Laughing out loud
- ROFL or ROTFL — Rolling on the floor laughing
- WRT — With regard to

Before you get carried away with expressions and gestures, remember that we must all mind our manners. Over the years, an etiquette (in this case Netiquette) has evolved. It's mostly common sense and treating others as you would like to be treated, just as you would do off-line.

I've included a list of the top ten points excerpted from *Netiquette*, by Virginia Shea from Albion Books on MSN. Some may seem rather esoteric, while others are obvious. They'll be discussed in more detail in the chapter on the Internet, as that is where they developed. Just remember the Golden Rule, and remember to share your knowledge!

1. Remember the human.
2. Adhere to the same standards of behavior on-line that you follow in real life.
3. Know where you are in cyberspace.
4. Respect other people's time and bandwidth.
5. Make yourself look good on-line.

6. Share expert knowledge.
7. Help keep flame wars under control.
8. Respect other people's privacy.
9. Don't abuse your power.
10. Be forgiving of other people's mistakes.

Clearing and Saving Chat Sessions for Review and Printing

Chat will automatically clear a chat window when it reaches a maximum length, prompting you to save the history first. If, on the other hand, you think the whole thing is a mess and want to clear the Chat History and start over, click Clear History from the Edit menu.

Saving a Chat Session

You can save your chat session, for later review or for printing.

1. From the File menu, select Save History.
2. To save all the formatting along with the text, make sure the file type is RTF (Rich Text Format).
3. Enter the name for the file. Click OK.

You can instruct chat sessions to be automatically saved when you exit a session. From the Tools menu select Options and then make sure Save Conversation History Before Clearing Or Exiting is checked.

Compose Pane

Below the History pane is the Compose pane. Here you type your message, make any changes you like, and click the Send button or press the Enter key. Keep in mind that the host is who designates you a spectator or a participant. If you are a spectator, you can observe but can't actually contribute or join the chat.

- If you need to start a new line, press Ctrl+Enter; if you want to indent a line, press Ctrl+Tab.
- Chat messages are not of an unlimited length. If your computer beeps at you while you are typing, you have probably reached the maximum length.

Members List Pane

Last is the Members List pane. This area lists the members who have entered the chat room and indicates whether they are participants, hosts, or spectators. To avoid confusion, you do have to see Spectators in the List. To show or hide them, from the View menu click Show Spectators.

- The host is an MSN member who moderates activity in a chat room and who you can contact via E-Mail. Not all chat rooms are moderated all the time, so don't expect to always see a host. If you don't see a host and need to contact someone about a forum, direct E-Mail to the Forum Manager instead.

While in a chat room, either observing or participating, you may want to find out more about a participating member. Double-click the person's name in the Member List pane to see the Member Properties. Or, highlight the member name and select Member Properties from the Tools menu.

Screening Chat Participants

If the Members List pane contains 15, 20, or more chat participants, you will find yourself having trouble keeping up with the thread of conversation you are following. You can have chat automatically screen out some members, leaving only those with whom you wish to converse.

1. In the Member List pane, click the names of the people you wish to screen out, leaving only those with whom you want to continue the chat.
2. From the View menu, click Ignore Members. Don't worry, you won't hurt anybody's feelings! Chat members can't tell when they're being ignored.
3. Make sure that Ignore Messages from Selected Members is checked. This option is available from the View menu.

Of course, if you want to ignore all but a few in a long list, this method would be tedious. Instead, invert the selection.

1. Click only the members you want to chat with in the Member List pane.
2. From the View menu select Ignore Members, then Invert Selection.
3. Click the View menu again, and select Ignore Members.
4. Make sure that Ignore Messages from Selected Members is checked.

Before you know it, you will know many people on-line with whom to chat. As you spend time in familiar chat rooms, you'll find yourself running into the same friends again and again, much as you would at your local coffee shop. Add them to your Personnel Address Book, and keep us all communicating!

CHAPTER 7

Bulletin Boards: Posting It to the Community

Every community has its bulletin boards. At the library, the corner store, and of course, the supermarket. Advertisements for used cars, baby-sitting, and apartments for rent abound. The on-line community is no different. They may be called newsgroups, forums, discussion groups, or message boards, but they are the community centers of the on-line village.

Are you looking for a long-lost relative, or just tracking the family tree? Try the genealogy bulletin board. People from all over the country, even all over the world can see your message and respond. And you are certainly not limited to asking and answering questions! Offer opinions, share some information, or even distribute helpful files.

Find a subject of interest, and browse through some of the messages. Post a response directly to the bulletin board, or have it automatically sent to the person's E-Mail address. This is the quickest way to meet people on-line (and perhaps less intimidating for a beginner than chat rooms), and you'll soon find yourself arranging to meet them in chat rooms.

But bulletin boards are so much more. Here is where you find the forums with an abundance of files to download. Files from independent content providers for free, files from ICPs for a charge, or files from other users that *exactly* suit your purpose. So let's continue our tour through the Microsoft Network and learn all the ways around its bulletin boards.

Reading and Printing Bulletin Board Messages

Bulletin boards are mainly found in the Categories area. Member Assistance has them as well, but they are obviously not dealing with the wide range of subject choices that you find in Categories, so let's begin there.

1. From MSN Central, click Categories.
2. Because various vendors in the computer industry put bulletin boards to such good use, we'll use them as an example. Double-click on the computers and software icon.
3. Moving further down the MSN Category tree, double-click the hardware folder icon.
4. Finally, click the Hardware BBS (bulletin board service) icon. Bulletin boards almost always are depicted by a framed square or rectangle and on it a note posted with a push-pin. These are sometimes partially obscured by a picture more specific to the topic at hand.
5. When the bulletin board window appears, it will be similar to the one in Figure 7.1. (If the toolbar is not visible, select Toolbar from the View menu.) Take a moment to look at the message list. Each message has a subject title, with an icon to the left. These icons indicate, with a plus or minus sign whether there is more

than the first message posted. A collection of connected messages is called a conversation.

A message may have neither a plus nor a minus sign, but a simple page. These are messages to which there have been no replies posted.

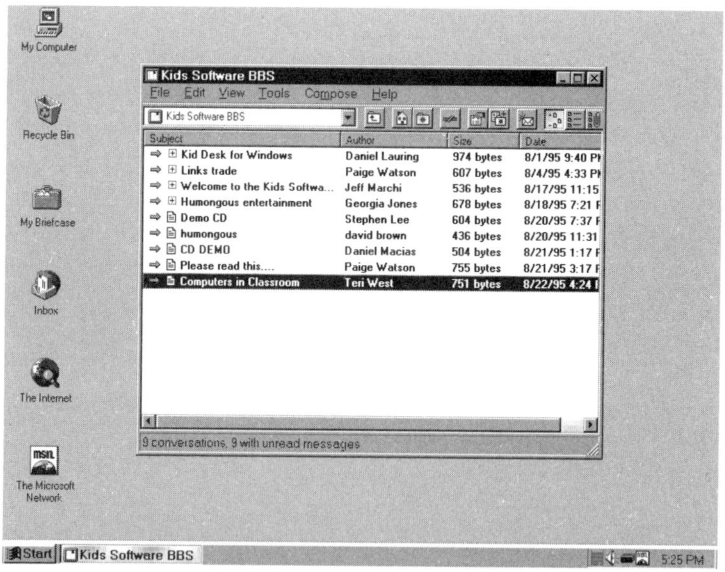

Figure 7.1 *A typical MSN bulletin board (BBS) window.*

- Clicking the + will list all the messages and replies in a conversation (Figure 7.2).
- To show only the messages in a conversation press Shift and click the + sign.
- After expanding the conversation, click the – sign to collapse it.

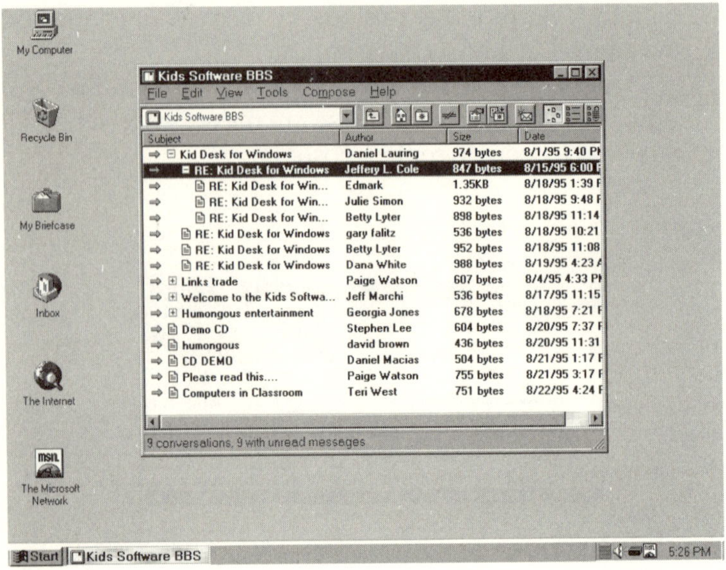

Figure 7.2 *The same window as Figure 7.1, but with one conversation fully expanded.*

To quickly expand *all* the conversations in the list, from the View menu click Expand All Conversations. To reverse the procedure, from the View menu select Collapse All Conversations.

Before selecting a conversation to read, you may want to see how many messages and replies it contains. If there are many conversations from which to choose, the number of messages in any one may be a deciding factor.

---

6. Double-click the message you wish to read. The message window will open and look similar to the one in Figure 7.3.

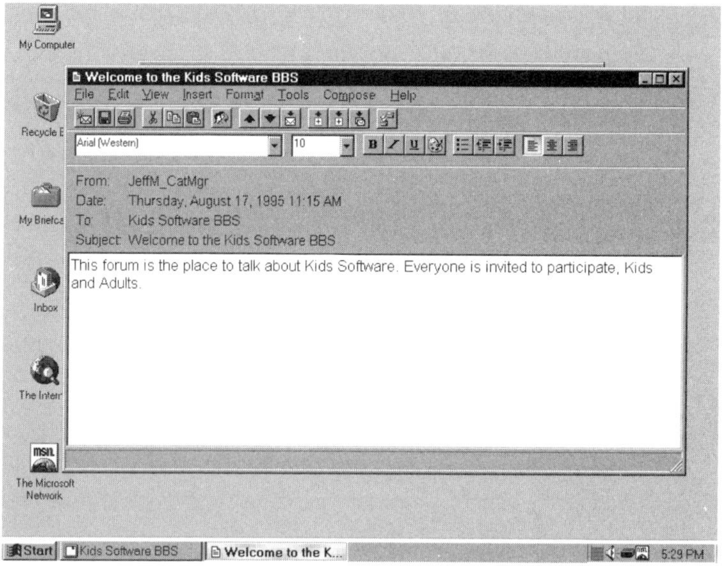

Figure 7.3 *An open bulletin board message. Messages can be automatically responded to, and a sender's address can be easily added to the Personal Address Book.*

7. Messages can be an all-text standard bulletin board message or include icons, usually with a description. These may be shortcuts to places you've never been or objects such as music, video clips, or graphics. Icons can also be linked to files that are available to you and the recipient or to files themselves that will be downloaded to your hard disk. Once the downloading begins you can move freely about doing other tasks, including checking the status of the file transfer (described below under File Transfer Status).
8. To read the next or previous message, click the up arrow or down arrow icon on the toolbar. This can also be accomplished by clicking the View menu and then selecting Next or Previous message.

The icon following the up and down arrows on the toolbar is used to read the next *unread* message, not necessarily the next message. Similarly, the next group of three icons are used to move up and down to the next conversation, and then down to the next *unread* conversation.

9. To print the message, click the File menu, and then Print, or click the printer icon.

You can display the member information as posted by the sender of the message. With the message open, double-click the member name and select Properties, or click the Tools menu and then click Member Properties.

Replying to a Bulletin Board Message

After reading the bulletin board messages, if you found an area of real interest you will want to send some replies. If the reply is an area of real general interest and of help to others and not personal, posting it to a bulletin board is the way to go.

1. With the message open, click the Compose menu.
2. Click Reply to BBS (Bulletin Board System).

The nature of your reply, or the nature of the original posting, may dictate the way you reply, for you are not limited to Reply to BBS. If it is of a more personal or individual nature (you finally found lost Uncle Walter!) use Reply by E-Mail or Forward by E-Mail.

---

3. Optionally, click the Subject area to give your reply a new description.
4. Click the message area and type in your reply.

5. Using the Insert menu, insert and attach files, provide links to files that are available to the recipient, and insert objects and shortcuts. These options are discussed in Chapter 5, Using E-Mail.
6. From the File menu, select Post Message.

Your bulletin board messages can reflect your thoughts and personality. Use the expressions and gestures listed in Chapter 6 on chatting. All of the formatting techniques described in Chapter 5, the E-Mail overview, are also available to you here. If the formatting toolbar is not available, from the View menu select Toolbar and then Formatting.

If you are thinking of responding to or printing a message, do it right away! MSN bulletin boards get a huge number of postings, and they cannot all appear on lists indefinitely. Once you exit a bulletin board any messages that have been read will not reappear when you return. Although in many cases, you *can* retrieve a previously read message by selecting the Tools menu and then clicking Show All Messages, forum managers have the option of disabling this feature, so you can never be certain a previously read message will still be there.

Other options on the Tools menu are Mark Message as Read, Mark Message as Unread, Mark Conversations as Read, and Mark Conversations as Unread. Using the mouse, you can mark individual messages to be included the next time you use the bulletin board. Or, by holding down the Ctrl key while you click with the mouse, you can mark multiple messages.

If you find a bulletin board becoming cluttered with tons of unread messages you know you will never read, select the last option on the Tools menu, Mark All Messages as Read. You will immediately notice that all the messages listed are no longer in bold face type and, after you exit and re-enter the board, all the messages will be gone.

Composing and Posting a New Bulletin Board Message

If after looking over the messages in a bulletin board you find none that deal with the subject hand, post a new message. Or, if you have a unique problem, ask a question of the community at large to get some help. This can be particularly useful in the computers and technology areas where you can ask a particular vendor questions about some difficulty you are having with a particular product. Your answer may come from the vendor, or another user may post the answer!

Of course you are not limited to computers and technology. Having problems with your car? Post it to the dealer! Need tips on slam-dunking? Shaquille O'Neal has a forum on-line.

1. Select the Category area with the appropriate bulletin board.
2. Open the bulletin board window where you wish to post a message.
3. Click the Compose menu, and then select New Message.

The New Message command is not always available. Some bulletin boards are Read-Only, with preselected postings and replies displayed.

4. In the Subject area, enter a brief description of the message.
5. Tab to the Message area and type your message. As described above in Replying to a Bulletin Board Message, all the additional formatting and insertion

features available to you in Microsoft Exchange E-Mail are available here.

6. From the File menu, click Post Message to post it to the bulletin board.

Postings usually take only a few minutes to appear, but they do not immediately go to the bulletin board. Delays are possible, so be patient!

File Transfer Status

The File Transfer Window is available from many spots in MSN under the Tools menu. But because bulletin boards are not only where we communicate by the written word, but also where we often exchange files of a significant size, it is discussed here. Every time you send or post a message with an attachment or copy the same, or download a file to your computer, a file is being transferred. If you are just posting the occasional E-Mail with a small attachment, this will be transparent. But if you are transferring large files frequently, the queue must be managed.

These files are then placed in a transfer queue where they can be manipulated at will. They can be put on hold or automatically copied the moment they are sent to the queue. You can change the order and the destination.

To begin, from the Tools menu select File Transfer Status. This will bring you to the window in Figure 7.4. Each file is listed with its name, size, the time it will take to transfer, its status, and its destination.

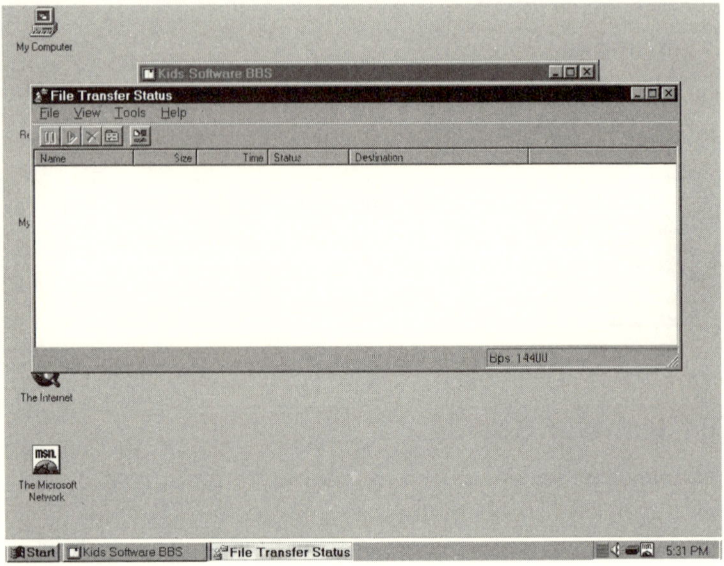

Figure 7.4 *The File Transfer Status window, where each file to be transferred can be managed.*

Holding Files in the Transfer Queue

Here files are listed in the order in which they were received. You cannot actually reorder the queue directly, but you can put individual files on hold, which will stop the transfer process.

1. Highlight the files you need to put on hold. Select multiple files by holding down the Ctrl key as you click each file.
2. From the File menu, click Pause.

Restarting File Transfer after Pause

1. Highlight the files you need to restart. Select multiple files by holding down the Ctrl key as you click each file.
2. From the File menu click Restart.

By using the Pause and Restart options you can reorder the file queue. Highlight the file you want to place at the top of the queue and select Pause from the File menu. Highlight the files in the order in which they should be transferred, clicking Pause after each selection. They will all be rearranged in the order in which they were put on hold.

Holding All Files in the Transfer Queue Automatically

Often you may not want files downloaded or uploaded as soon as they are requested. Although a transfer is a background operation, it does use system resources and may slow things down; it may also just not be convenient.

1. From the Tools menu select Options or click the Options icon on the toolbar.
2. The dialog box in Figure 7.5 appears.

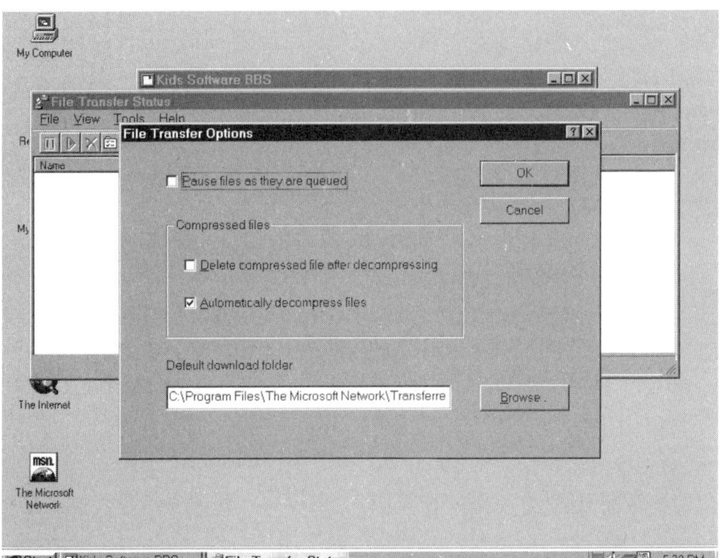

Figure 7.5 *The File Transfer Status Options available from the menu, the toolbar, or Ctrl+O.*

Removing Files from the Transfer Queue

If you ever look at the File Transfer Status window in bewilderment ("Whatever could I have been thinking!"), all is not lost.

1. Highlight the file to be removed.
2. From the File menu click Remove.

You can also remove a file that has already begun to transfer.

1. Highlight the file name that has begun the transfer.
2. From the File menu select Pause.
3. Select the File menu again, and click Remove.

File Transfer and Compression

To save time and money most long files are transferred after they have been compressed. MSN fully supports file compression and gives you two options for dealing with the files once they have been transferred. Should the files be automatically decompressed after transfer? If they are, should the compressed file be automatically deleted after transfer?

1. From the Tools menu select Options.
2. In the dialog box shown in Figure 7.5 check the appropriate boxes.
3. If the Automatically Decompress Files box is *not* checked, the files will not be decompressed at transfer. You will have to decompress them later and delete the compressed file yourself.
4. If the Delete Compressed File after Decompressing box is *not* checked, the compressed files will not be deleted at transfer. The file will be decompressed with the original compressed file also left in place.

Changing Default File Destinations

When the Microsoft Network Software is initially installed, it sets up a default folder for transferred file. The default folder is usually C:\Program Files\The Microsoft Network\Transferred Files, which may be totally inappropriate for you!

1. From the Tools menu select Options.
2. When the dialog box in Figure 7.5 appears, type in the folder name and path you would like for your files.

If you are unsure, or just don't want to type, click the browse button and choose your location.

Automatic Disconnect after File Transfer

If File Transfer is the only MSN service you are using at the time, MSN can automatically sign you off when you are finished. If however, you are uploading or downloading while chatting, reading your mail, or merely browsing, this will have no effect.

When you are transferring a large file or number of files, you may not need to keep track of when the transfer is complete or you may simply need to be away from your computer, doing something else entirely.

1. In the File Transfer Status window click the File menu.
2. Click Transfer and Disconnect.

Bulletin boards are rapidly becoming the support option of choice for many computer vendors. As the use of on-line services increases, I suspect that this trend will widen. But for now, make use of them for business when you need and for fun whenever you can. They can lead to increased productivity as well as expanding horizons. Have fun!

CHAPTER 8

Categories—The Heart and Soul of MSN

Sure, E-Mail improves your communications but categories are really what it's all about—the sheer wealth of available information, in every conceivable format, that makes an online service compelling. Here, on the Categories page of MSN, is where you find the forums (bulletin boards, chat rooms, conferences, and file libraries) that define the real content of MSN.

Categories include everything from stock quotations to parenting tips to education. But it's not all serious by any means. There are tips on such games as Doom to Monopoly and live question and answer sessions with rock stars and chefs, sports heroes, and computer gurus.

Currently, MSN is divided into these broad categories:

- Arts & Entertainment
- Business & Finance
- Community & Public Affairs
- Computers & Software
- Home & Family

- News & Weather
- Science & Technology
- Sports, Health, & Fitness

Each of these communities break down into more and more specific areas. If you look at Figure 8.1, you will see that the main Categories window includes many more categories than the eight listed here, and double-clicking any folder icon will always bring you a new window with a more narrowly defined selection. For example, double-clicking the Science & Technology icon opens the window shown in Figure 8.2, with its own collection of folder icons.

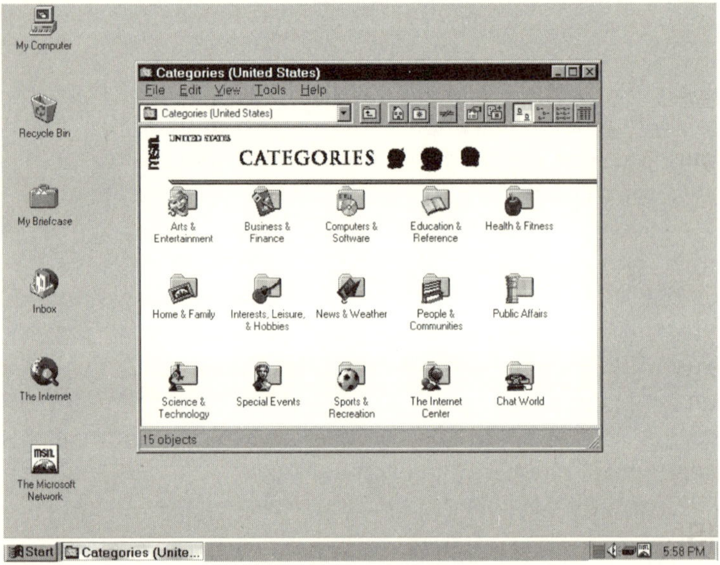

Figure 8.1 *MSN's main Category window. From here you can go to the hundreds of forums, chat rooms, and bulletin boards available on the Microsoft Network and over the Internet.*

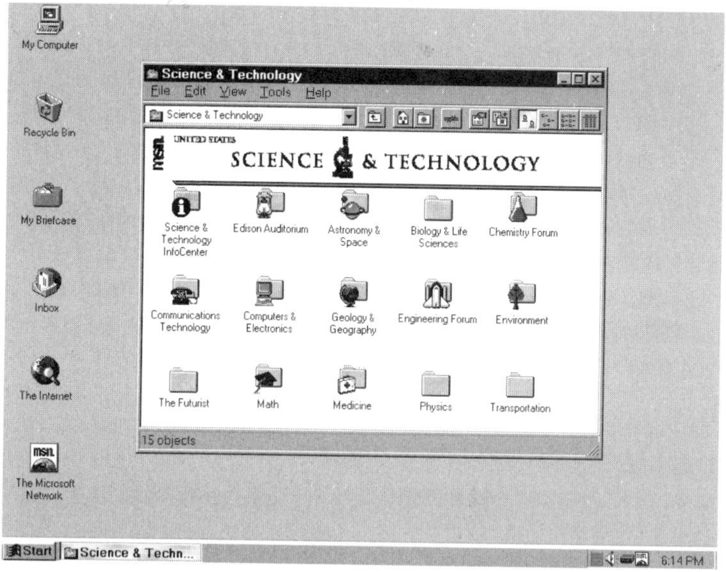

Figure 8.2 *Each category in Figure 8.1 has more specific folders associated with it.*

As you move along, remember that icons are often duplicated and forums seen in more than one place. Don't be led into thinking that these are different areas entirely. A forum may be a good fit for different areas, and because an icon only represents, or points to, a particular forum, bulletin board, chat room, or whatever, it is one of those rare things that can be in two places at once.

MSN Icons and What They May (and May Not) Symbolize

MSN category area icons try to be consistent, to better allow you to know what direction to take when exploring or looking for a particular subject or type of forum. Keep in mind, though, that the forum managers at MSN are nothing if not creative. Expect that an icon may be partially obscured by or superimposed on another graphic that more closely relates to the category subject.

- **Folder icons** Folder icons are where you will always begin, they are the top level of every category grouping. Beneath each there may be nothing but more folder icons, but each one of these will be the top of its own tree of topics and icons, each in turn more particular to the topic named at the top of the category window (Figure 8.2). Eventually you will reach a more varied window. There may yet be more folder icons leading down yet more paths, but there will be other types as well, each pertaining to that window's category (Figure 8.3).

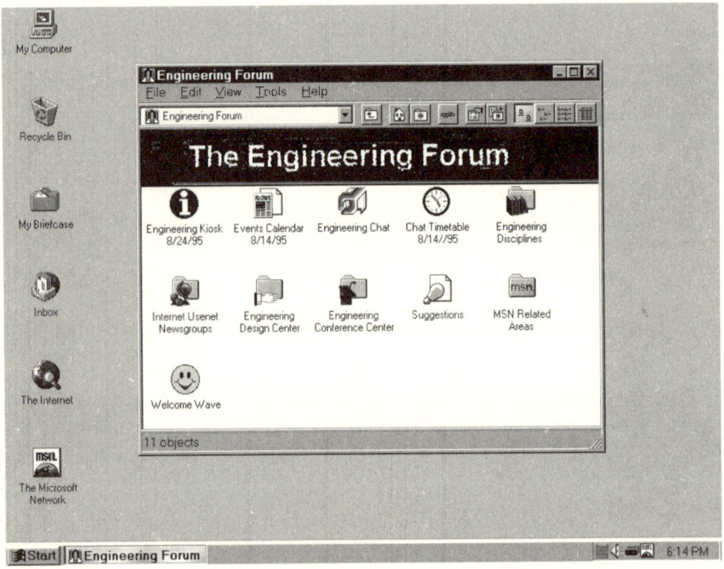

Figure 8.3 *Every category subject has a range of icon types from which to choose.*

- **Kiosk icons** Kiosks are general information centers in the shape of a circle with the letter "i" in the center. The first icon in Figure 8.3 is a Kiosk. They are usually files that are downloaded to your computer (often opening a word-processor or another editor such as

WordPad) to be saved, printed, or both. These files are updated regularly and include timely information applicable to a particular forum. There may be several different Kiosks in a category, each at different levels covering that level's particular information needs.

- **Bulletin boards** Bulletin boards are usually depicted by a framed square with a paper and push-pin on it. Like other icons, all bulletin board icons are not exactly alike, but may be combined with other graphics to more closely resemble its subject.

In many areas on the Microsoft Network you will find bulletin boards represented by a bulletin board icon with a box in front stuffed with pieces of paper. These are suggestion boxes, put there for the express purpose of user input. Forum managers are always looking for tips on how to improve their offerings in order to make MSN as lively and interesting as possible. Don't be shy, it's for everyone's benefit!

- **Chat room icons** Chat rooms are illustrated with a comic-strip type talk balloon. If it is a small chat room meant for private chats, its title will often include its size. If you are unsure, check out its Properties.
- **Download & Run icons** Depending on the forum, these icons vary in appearance but always send a file to your computer. It will either be self-containing and run on its own, or will instruct another program on your hard disk, such as an editor or word processor, to open and use the file. Bear in mind that as consistent as MSN tries to be, there are limitations to how much an icon can tell you. Looking at Figure 8.3 again, notice that both Events Calendar and Suggestions have pieces of paper in their icons. But the Calendar simply downloads a document while Suggestions downloads a program that asks for input then transmits that input to the appropriate party.

- **Binocular icon** To help you find your way around not only MSN but the World Wide Web as well, double-clicking the Binocular icon will bring up a sponsored "siteseeing" guide. This is an interactive screen with all of the main MSN categories listed on the left, and different Web sites, appropriate to the category selected, portrayed on the right. You have the option of clicking the illustrated buttons to get more information, or if you have Internet access privileges, of going directly to the site itself. If you do not have access privileges, there will be a button with helpful information on how to get it.

As you travel up and down the different levels of folders, you may feel as though you'll never find your way back again. Remember, when you finally find what you are looking for, think of Favorite Places.

Adding Icons to Your Favorite Places Folder

I can't tell you the number of times I've "lost" a place I really liked. It *seemed* like a business subject, so it must be there, only it's not. Or I remembered the topic, but was it a forum or only a subject on the Bookshelf? Of course I found it eventually—by searching up and down categories, or finally using Find. But if you use something frequently or just think you may use it frequently, put it in your Favorite Places folder. That way it is always easily accessible each time you sign on or from the MSN Indicator icon on the task bar.

Losing your place is not the only reason to maintain a Favorite Places folder. Once you are an MSN regular you will find yourself developing a routine. First News and Weather, then the Sports reports, Stocks, and finally stopping in for your favorite evening chat. Having everything in one convenient place will help automate the process.

You don't put the actual service, forum, or bulletin board in your Favorite Places folder, but only the icon that takes you there.

1. Find the forum, chat room, bulletin board, or anything that you want to add to your Favorite Places folder. This can be in the Categories area or Member Assistance.
2. Highlight the icon representing the service by clicking on it.
3. From the File menu click Add to Favorite Places.

If you are already in the service, there is no need to exit. You can click Add to Favorite Places from the File menu directly.

Removing an Icon from Favorite Places

1. Open your Favorite Places folder from MSN Central.
2. Highlight the icon to be removed.
3. From the File menu select Delete.

Displaying a Forum's Properties

Despite MSN's efforts to have each icon indicate what's up, you may not always be able to tell what you'll find. To save time you can get a brief description of the folder or other area types by looking at its Properties box.

Properties

Figure 8.4 shows a typical Properties box. It contains not only a description, but also provides a rating (such as a movie release would have), indicates the size of the file, and states if there is an additional price associated with it.

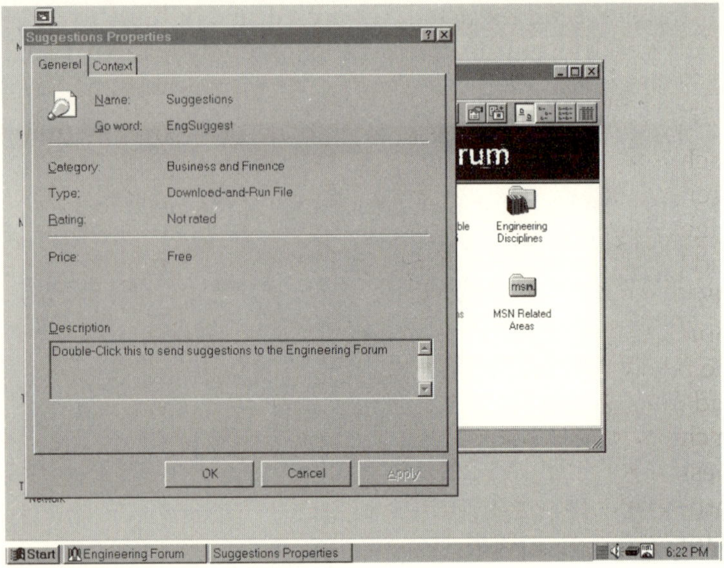

Figure 8.4 *An icon's Property box lists certain facts about it and offers a brief description.*

1. Highlight the icon for which you need additional information.
2. Click the Properties icon on the toolbar (the hand holding a piece of paper), right-click, and select Properties from the menu that appears, or select Properties from the File menu.

The General tab in the Properties box gives most of the information you'll usually need about a forum. If you'll be returning often, make note of its Go word. If it's a file you'll be downloading, make note of its price. And if it's a folder you're just investigating, take a look at the description, and you'll have a better idea of what comes next.

The Context tab gives more specific information about the highlighted area. Here you can find out who the forum manager is and who the owner is, what topics are covered, to whom it is directed and in what language. Also listed is where in the MSN scheme of things it is (category or folder), its size, when it was created and when it was last changed.

Forum Managers

Each community is led by a forum manager. Forum managers are experts in their field, bringing specialized knowledge and insight. They generally monitor the chat rooms and bulletin boards to ensure that they are in line with MSN policies and that the content is pertinent to the forum topic. A forum manager will schedule conferences, manage the file library, set guidelines unique to a particular forum and designate who are spectators and who are participators in chat rooms. Often they will respond to bulletin board messages or chats, and, if you have any questions about a forum, you can direct them to the forum manager. Finally, it is forum managers who bring focus to a community, setting the tone of the environment.

You too can become a forum manager. If you are interested, send a message to sysop@msn.com.

Make MSN Your Own

So jump in and enjoy, for it is in Categories that you will be doing the most exploring. And the more you use MSN the more it will be yours. Independent content providers will be looking to members for feedback on not just their products, but on their forums as well, while the MSN forum managers are always looking to make MSN more of a community for all of us.

And last, don't let your environment (or your Favorite Places folder) become static, for every day there are new forums added, new magazines published, new products covered.

CHAPTER 9

Arts & Entertainment

Arts & Entertainment (Figure 9.1) covers a wide range of subjects: movies, the theater, art and design, television and radio, comedy, humor, music, and comics and animation. Also included are traditional forms of the print media: books, newspapers, and magazines.

Art & Design

Art & Design covers the main design areas: architecture, photography, fine arts, computer design and graphics, and the like.

The Photography forum is a fairly typical and rich one (Figure 9.2). It consists of many bulletin boards and chat rooms covering different disciplines including, but not limited to, general photography, the art of photography, professional photography, and the photo industry news. There are separate, dedicated forums devoted to film paper and darkroom supplies, and there are Photo Usenet Groups. ICPs have started their own forums, with thousands of images available to download.

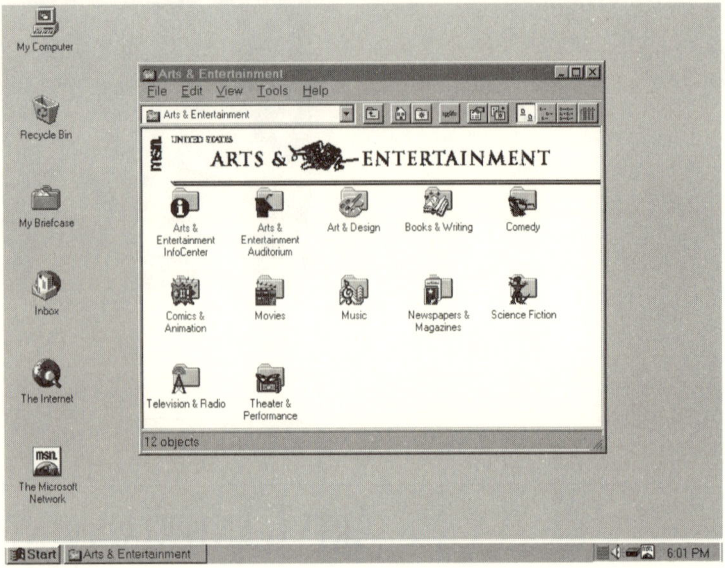

Figure 9.1 *The Arts & Entertainment category has forums on a surprisingly broad range of subjects.*

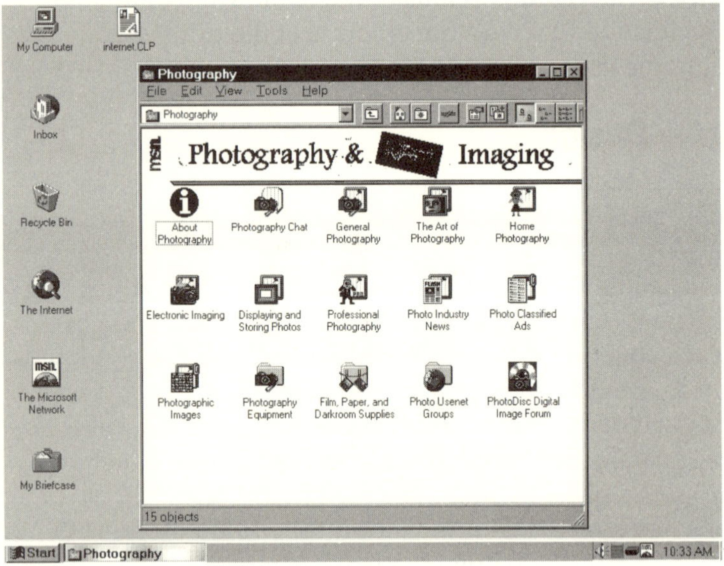

Figure 9.2 *The Photography forum has areas for everything dealing with photography.*

Artline Forum

The Artline forum is for those interested in the fine arts. You will find separate areas for discussion of both well known and lesser known works, and there are forums devoted to the larger issues of the art world and the art market.

And let's not forget the galleries! Visit them to your heart's content and keep in mind that you can download many of the images.

Computer Design & Graphics

Computer design is an exciting, new field. Well, new compared to the rest of the arts. And because it is so obviously connected to the computer world, you will find a lot of online support and fellow designers. The most popular graphics software vendors have forums for both discussion and support, and many lesser known ones are here as well.

Books & Writing

When it comes to books there are really only two areas to be concerned with, one for reading and one for writing. And when you think about it, what else is there to do with books?

There is a forum for writers that has separate forums devoted to new writers and student writers aged 13 to 18, a special area for kids, and forums for tools and resources.

Take a look at the Reading forum, which has different chat rooms and bulletin boards for discussing best sellers and classics alike.

Comedy

Look up the Comedy Connection forum for a few laughs. Here you'll find jokes and stories for kids of all ages. Bulletin boards and chat rooms, forums for jokes, puns and limericks, humor in the media, kids, and, of course, an adult humor area called Adult Fun House. The Fun House can be accessed only by an adult over 18 who has transmitted a special release.

For the more serious side of things, those in the comedy profession have an area their own called the Comedy Professional BBS.

Comics & Animation

Everybody loves or loved to read the comics, and we all still admire fine animation. Forums here contain live animation, special events, and bulletin boards and chat rooms for special favorites. In the Parents Council you will find reviews of comics by age ranges and topic.

Movies

The Movies forum is really special. The advanced technology of MSN allow ICPs to do some really neat things. Hollywood On-line has not only the expected chat rooms and bulletin boards but movie trailers as well. Now, when you are trying to decide what to see on a Saturday night, check out the trailers of current movies, not just the old movie clips that have been available for a while now.

The Multimedia Library is also pretty cool. Different forums provide not only trailers and information on hot new movies, but clips of sounds, photos, tools, and interactive kits.

If you're into the movie scene, don't forget Mr. Showbiz. Be dazzled by celebrity interviews, the latest entertainment news, gossip, box office grosses, and reviews.

Music

No matter your taste in music, there is a forum here to delight you. Separate areas dedicated to classical, rock, folk, blues, and jazz are here. For the guitar lovers among you, there is even a separate forum for you. Forums contain not only the usual chat rooms and bulletin boards, but also reference rooms, news stories, record buyers tip sheets, lists of top recordings, and forums dedicated to your favorite recording artist. For the electronic music enthusiast there is a separate forum with tips and tricks of the trade. For the really sick among you, don't forget the latest list of Who's Who of Rap Artists in Jail.

News & Magazines

Nothing can replace the printed page but certainly there is a lot that can augment it. Major magazine publishers are on-line with discussion groups in chat rooms and can communicate directly with authors and editors. There are regular columns, feature articles, some original video and audio clips, and summaries of articles that have appeared in printed form.

If you decide to subscribe, subscription forms can be downloaded to be filled in and then automatically transmitted via Microsoft Exchange to the publisher.

Science Fiction

The Science Fiction category actually covers both science fiction and fantasy. Meet people to talk to about favorite books and authors or check out Fandom, where you'll find like-minded fantasy enthusiasts. There is a separate forum for all science fiction and fantasy not found in books but in both movies and television.

Television & Radio

Whether your taste runs to drama, soaps, or news, this is the place. There are bulletin boards for every genre, with a separate forum for those explosive TV dramas otherwise known as televised celebrity trials.

In this video world of seeing is believing, let's not forget radio. National Public Radio has its own bulletin board, and there are forums for radio engineering, programming, promotion, production, and, last but certainly not least, listening.

Theater & Performance

Theater & Performance is a forum with many colors. It consists not only of forums dedicated to the theater as we traditionally think of it but also to any performing art, including acting, dance, opera, magic, and musical theater. There are special events with actors, dancers, and other performers as well as theatrical libraries. Performers can find information on upcoming conventions and access a variety of information resources.

CHAPTER 10

Business & Finance

No matter the size, nature, or location of your business or whether your financial needs are personal or professional, the Business & Finance category (Figure 10.1) has something for you. Covering areas such as banking and investing and providing business news and reference tools, the Business & Financial category is all-inclusive.

If you're frustrated because you've located and then lost a forum that blends perfectly with your business or finance needs, don't despair. Even if you have not put it into your Favorite Places folder or made note of its Go word, the forum managers have taken into account that this is a category that is rich and varied and constantly evolving. There are so many interrelated forums, and so many that don't seem to fit neatly into any one area, that they have created a special directory just for this category. The Business & Finance Directory folder contains multiple folders, each containing all the other folders in the category, this time grouped alphabetically.

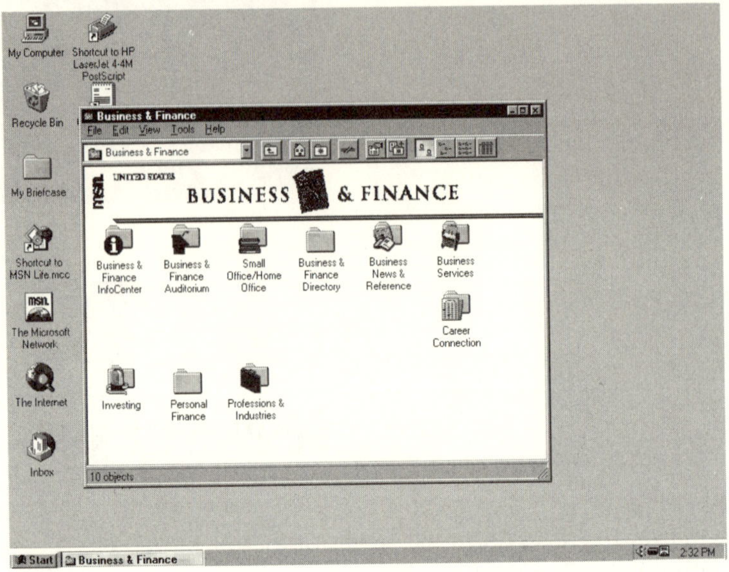

Figure 10.1 *The Business & Finance category covers every aspect of the business and financial communities.*

Small Business/Home Office

It used to be that one of the hardest things about running a small business was the lack of tools that the big guys had. No longer. MSN puts everything you need at your finger-tips (well, at your mouse tips). Not just reference tools from Dun & Bradstreet, the American Management Association, the Small Business Administration, and the like, but also tips on how to save money and information on changes in the law that can affect your business. You are also able to exchange information, tips, and encouragement with other business people—other business people in your field sharing your needs and concerns.

For the start-up, there are guides for the entrepreneur. There is also help to be had on finding venture capital and on starting a business from scratch.

Careers

In this changing economy it is always wise to nurture your career. Business and Finance provides not just career opportunities on-line, but training and counseling as well. There is special counseling (private, if need be) available for those who have lost their jobs or been fired. Then, when it all works out, turn here for relocation information!

Investing

Investing on-line should be much more than a stock quote service, and MSN delivers. Stock quotes are available here but so are the real tools of the trade. Get on-line market reviews and trend analysis, receive information on new stocks, trade tips and investment strategies with other investors, and get up-to-the-minute tax information. You can access directories that identify all the corporations on the NASDAQ and the NYSE, but it doesn't stop there. There are directories of corporations sponsoring direct stock purchase plans and directories of corporations with Web sites on the Internet.

This area is really one where you have to take some time to explore and to find the tools that work best for you. Most of the ICPs here who charge for their service have a free trial offer of some kind, a newsletter sample, or a time trial to help you learn, pick, and choose.

Professions & Industries

Every industry and profession has its own ways—ways of doing things, its own dialog, its own newsletters, and, on MSN, its own forum. These professions now include, but are not limited to, accounting, advertising, design and public relations, banking and finance, civil service, communications and entertainment, hospitality and travel, human resources, law, medicine, real estate, sales, marketing and management, science and engineering, and insurance.

If your profession is not on the list, that doesn't mean it isn't present. It may be part of another forum, just as the Television & Radio forum can be found here in the Communications & Entertainment forum *and* in the Radio Professional forum in the Arts & Entertainment category. If you don't see it on the above list, and more important if you don't see it on the screen (there are new forums added all the time), use Find before you decide that what you are looking for is not around.

International Trade

Those whose business is international have special concerns. Concerns with tariffs, shipping schedules, and just plain time. What time of day is it? And how much time will it take to travel and ship such distances? The International Trade forum addresses these needs with conferences, trade show directories, newsletters, and standard trade directories. Shipping providers such as Federal Express and the United Parcel Service are a presence here for tracking purposes and general account information.

Personal Finance

Many of the services offered in the investment forums are offered here, including information on bond, electronic banking, accounting, and brokerage houses. But there is more here that especially addresses the personal finance needs of individual users.

If you've ever purchased a home you know how frustrating it can be to secure a mortgage. Well, with MSN you can go through the whole process on-line. There are complete instructions for filling out the application and on how best to get approved. And it all comes with live interest rates so you can shop around!

If it's taxes you're worried about (aren't we all?), stop by the Accounting forum. You'll find chat rooms and bulletin boards, and a directory of accountants if you need to find one. And for the accountants among us, there is a Continuing Education forum as well as forums dedicated to each of the accounting areas of specialization.

Perhaps the biggest change to come to money management in the home over the last few years has been the easy-to-use money management software such as Microsoft Money, Quicken, and others. Come to their forums to learn about new features and about existing ones you never knew were there. Come to ask questions of the experts from the tech support field and other users.

CHAPTER 11

Computers & Software

As the vision of a computer on every desktop becomes a reality, so too grows the on-line services tech support market, with an ever-increasing number of bulletin boards providing hardware and software support. In fact, it may be that vendor-supported bulletin boards contributed directly to the phenomenal growth of on-line services, as this type of support is often superior to that which you can get any other way. The Microsoft Network is no exception (Figure 11.1). Ask questions directly of the people who wrote the software and of the people who support it. All this without expensive phone charges and long waiting periods while placed on hold.

Often as good and sometimes even better is the additional support you receive from other users. As you yourself no doubt have observed, you never really learn how to use a software package or install a piece of hardware until you have to. You can take all the courses in the world, read all the manuals and books that are out there, but you have to use it to learn it.

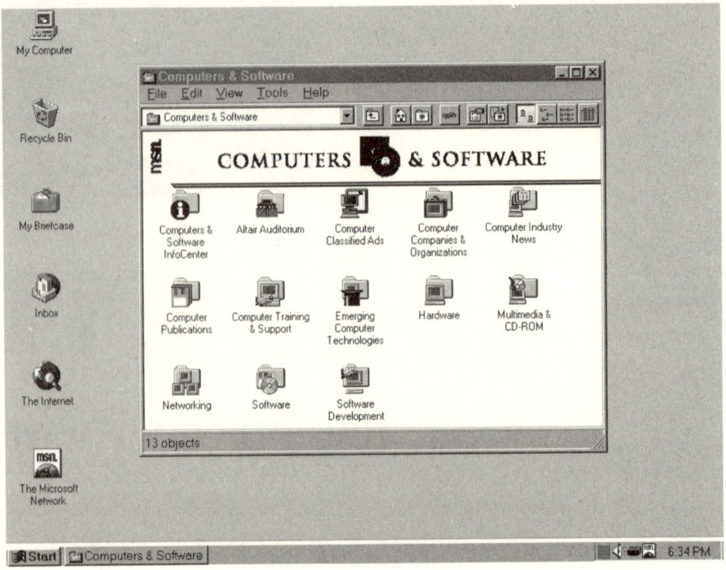

Figure 11.1 *The Computers & Software category is for both vendors and users alike.*

Other users have gone through a learning curve similar to yours, including taking those courses and having those same books on hand. They may have tried to get software to jump through the same hoops or may have experienced the same difficulties installing particularly troublesome hardware. When you post a question to a bulletin board, you never know who may respond. It may be the vendor with a fix for the problem or a user with a different software or hardware solution altogether.

Hardware Manufacturers

Along with forums of the major PC manufacturers, you'll find forums of manufacturers of peripheral devices such as modems and printers and of add-ons such as video boards, disk drives, and tape back-up units. These forums are not just user bulletin boards, but are a treasure trove of information from many sources. There are product information forums with price sheets, specification sheets, and press releases.

Files

For many, the most useful feature are the downloadable files. A piece of computer hardware or software doesn't have to be on the store shelves for very long before the drivers it is shipped with have been made obsolete. Obsolete long before you even got it home! When you try and try and just cannot figure out why the darn thing will not work, post the problem on the vendor's bulletin board. What you may get back for an answer are instructions to download a file from the vendor's file library and your troubles will be over! Well, your hardware troubles, anyway.

Software

Hardware may be useful, but software's where the fun is. There are lots and lots of software vendors (Figure 11.2) offering support on MSN, and the support is not all business. There are special forums for software developers themselves to ask questions of each other, for multimedia and CD ROM products, and for emerging computer technologies.

Many of the points made in the hardware section above about bulletin boards and support hold true here. When you hit a wall, and just cannot figure out what to do next, contact the vendor on MSN and you'll soon get an answer.

And as with the hardware forums, there are new product announcements. But because you are so much more involved with every nuance of how a piece of software looks, feels, and behaves, new product announcements are more exciting and avidly awaited. Further, the results are more gratifying. Because you are communicating directly with the creators of the software, they rely on you for user feedback, often making the determination of what or what not to include with a new release or product on the basis of what they hear on-line.

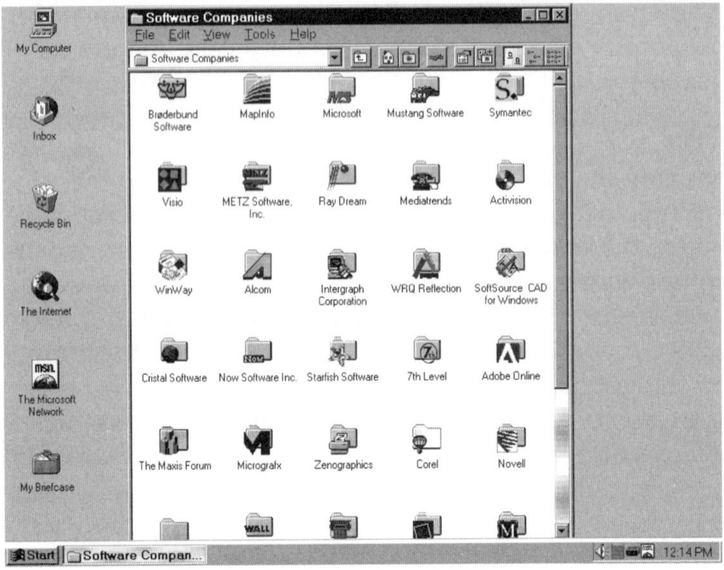

Figure 11.2 *The Software Companies forum has a vast array of companies represented.*

Business Software

Business software support covers a wide range, from the usual office products such as word processing, spreadsheets, graphics, and statistical packages to the software forums of hardware manufacturers. There are forums from the leading networking companies (where you'll really need some help) and from software utility manufacturers to help you get the most out of all the stuff you've already got. Don't be afraid to ask questions here; these forums are for beginners and the experienced alike, with each group learning from the other.

Game Software

Game software has certainly got its appeal. Here are special forums with hints for those impossible fantasy games. No matter how many maps you've drawn, no matter how many nights you've been up until 3:00 a.m., it seems you just can't solve the puzzle. MSN comes to the rescue with forums devoted exclusively to individual games, hosted by the creators of the software.

Publications

Not all of the computer industry is hardware and software. There are publications dedicated to covering everything going on in hardware and software, and there are periodicals dedicated to everything having to do with the computer industry itself. These are the most popular PC publications available. Their on-line formats differ from their printed versions, with easier access to just the information you need made possible. There are the slick PC publications of Ziff Davis on through to Computer Shopper, where mail-order shopping is king. Take some time to browse through them, noticing how they differ, what each offers, and what is the price for each as an on-line service. You will find them invaluable when making purchase decisions, as finding independent product reviews and recommendations has never been more effortless.

Education

Whether computers are your profession or the tools you use to reach other goals, it seems that there is never enough time to learn all that you need to know about them. Or when you do have the time, it seems that the course offerings are off in another city or state hundreds of miles away. MSN has an alternative with a wide range of computer education choices.

If you're interested in learning more about Microsoft products, take some time to wander through the campus of the Microsoft Online Institute (MOLI). Whatever you expect to find on a college campus, you'll find here. Start out with an orientation session or drop by the Student Union. In addition to classrooms where instructors not only bring you up to speed on Microsoft products but also enable you to become a certified Microsoft Developer, you'll find chat rooms to meet other students and instructors, a campus bookstore not limited to enrolled students, a library, and an administration building. To answer question about what course of study is best for you, drop into the Advising forum to meet with a guidance counselor, look at a course catalog, or just find out the best person to meet with.

Computer education is not limited to the Microsoft product line. There are newsletters and courses on many other manufacturers' products. Application software, operating environments, and networking topics are covered in depth. This coverage is not always provided by the software or hardware vendor. There are third party support forums from those who have been involved with computer training and support for many years and have now transferred that expertise to the on-line world.

CHAPTER 12

Education & Reference

The Education & Reference category is a multipurpose one (Figure 12.1). It has extensive education forums for those wishing to take courses on a variety of subjects, it has reference tools for students of every discipline, and it serves those in the education community as well.

College Preparation

For those bound for college or graduate school there are numerous preparation courses for the SATs, GSATs, LSATs, and the like. These courses have been offered for years around the country, but now they can be taken in the convenience of your home. They can vastly improve your scores and thereby vastly improve your chances of getting into the school of your choice.

More than just presenting dry information on the standardized tests, these forums can get pretty lively. There are forums with advice on undergraduate and grad school selection and admissions. And once you do get accepted by the school of your choice, look for advice on acquiring

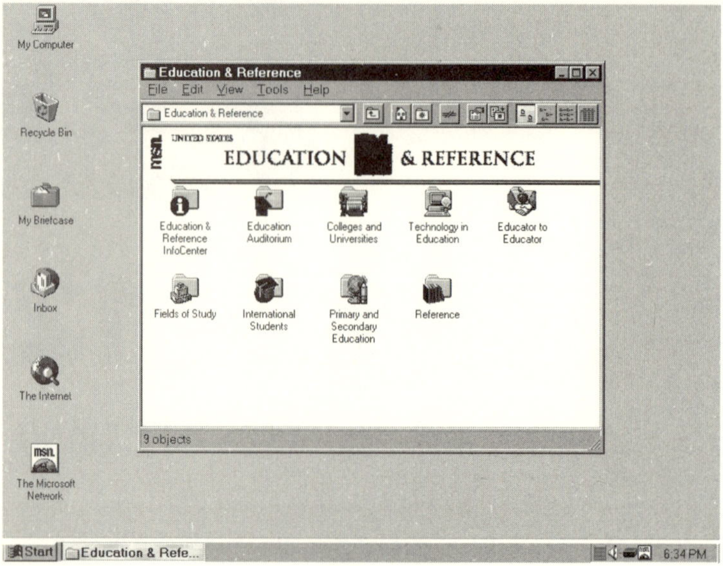

Figure 12.1 *The Education & Reference category gives alternatives in education and a vast array of resource tools.*

financial aid and tips on improving studying habits. From the bulletin boards you can download files as you need them. But you're not left on your own entirely. Stop in the auditoriums where there are chat workshops and tutorials.

Fields of Study

All over the Microsoft Network in almost every category you'll find on-line courses. In the Arts & Entertainment category there are courses on the fine arts and writing, and in Science & Technology there are courses on geology and geography. The Education & Reference category strives to gather all of these together under one roof. Some may have been missed though. If what you are looking for is not here, go directly to a category more closely associated with the subject, or use Find if you still cannot track it down.

Along with a particular course comes its attending forums with bulletin boards and chat rooms. The more you learn, the more you'll enjoy conversing with people in the chat rooms associated with your subject, helping others on the bulletin boards and getting help yourself.

International Education

If you are interested in studying abroad or hosting a foreign exchange student, spend some time in the International Student Forum. You'll find complete "How To" information on becoming a foreign exchange student yourself or qualifying as a host family.

Future foreign exchange students can meet prospective families in chat rooms to talk about a different country's customs and culture or just get to know each other. There are forums where pre- and post-exchange students can establish Pen Pal relationships with present foreign exchange students and with each other.

Today there are many independent foreign exchange services available to the prospective exchange student and host family. Use the International forum to gather information for help in determining which is the best one for each individual.

An unusual on-line service that is available here concerns language translation software, with forums that review software and make software available for review. For the homesick there are phone tools and tips for keeping in touch with a family far away.

Teachers Talk to Teachers

It's tough coming up with new ideas day after day when you're trying to teach. Students seem smarter today, or maybe it's just that technology is changing so fast. But now you don't have to do it all on your own. Here there are forums just for the innovative teacher. Discover new products to make your job easier and more rewarding or discover some that have been out there but unknown to you. Learn about other teachers' imaginative lesson plans and share some of your own. Talk about your experience with stories and activities—those that work and those that don't!

But don't think that the forums in the educator's areas are for teachers only. There are sites for administrators, librarians, and coaches. Share not only your ideas, but your frustrations as well. You may find some answers on MSN, or check out the Smart Links folder where related Internet sites are found.

Reference

Computers and reference tools—what a wonderful marriage. The research that used to take hours, if not days or weeks, can now be accomplished in minutes. When you think of on-line reference tools, think of your local library where you'll find not only books but monthly, weekly, and daily periodicals too.

USA Today Life (USATLife) features entertainment and health coverage and an expanded version of the popular USA Today Best-Selling Books list. Unlike the newspaper's printed version, this computer edition has an innovative daily interactive crossword puzzle that can be played at different skill levels.

Here in the reference forum you'll also find the more traditional books: encyclopedias, dictionaries, thesauruses, and atlases.

Microsoft Bookshelf and Encarta are good examples. These are introductory versions of the CD ROM products available for sale. Bookshelf is a collection of three: a dictionary, thesaurus, and atlas. With just a click of the mouse, you can look up a topic or word in one of the volumes or in all of them (Figure 12.2). Encarta is a full-featured encyclopedia that can be searched by an individual word within an article, by category to find a certain area of interest, or with

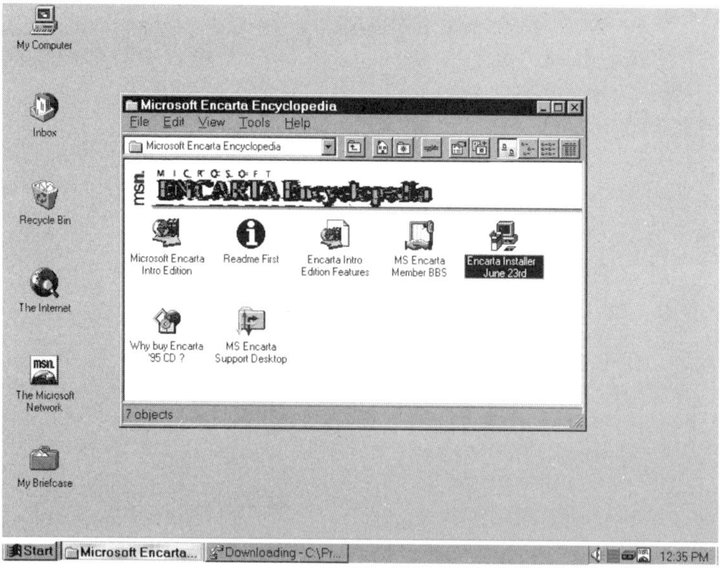

Figure 12.2 *The Microsoft Encarta encyclopedia is as easy to use as it is to install. While installation is going on, the computer can be put to other tasks.*

an image filter to find only those articles that contain pictures and maps. To really fine-tune the search, use all three search criteria.

Although these introductory versions are very useful, they are limited when compared to the versions for sale. There are no full-motion video clips, no sound clips, and no animation. As far as sheer functionality goes, they lack the full integration with standard application software, such as word processing, spreadsheet, and presentation software packages, that their CD ROM counterparts have. But they're a great way to get started exploring the range of reference resources!

CHAPTER 13

Health & Fitness

Forums related to health and fitness abound on the Microsoft Network. Although recreational sports contribute to a sense of physical well-being, the Health & Fitness category contains all the topics that are *not* related to any specific recreational activity (Figure 13.1). There are forums for the health professional as well as forums for the non-professional interested only in maintaining his or her own health.

Exercise & Physical Fitness

Jump right in, the step aerobic class is just starting! Seriously though, while no on-line activity is a substitute for a good workout, there are forums here that will help you get the most out of the workouts you do get in, at home, in the gym, or outdoors. Here are bulletin boards devoted to all forms of exercise (including one just for aerobics).

Check out the Exercise Equipment and Facilities bulletin board for valuable information and user input on using and buying cardiovascular exercise and monitoring devices, general fitness machines, and cross-country equipment such

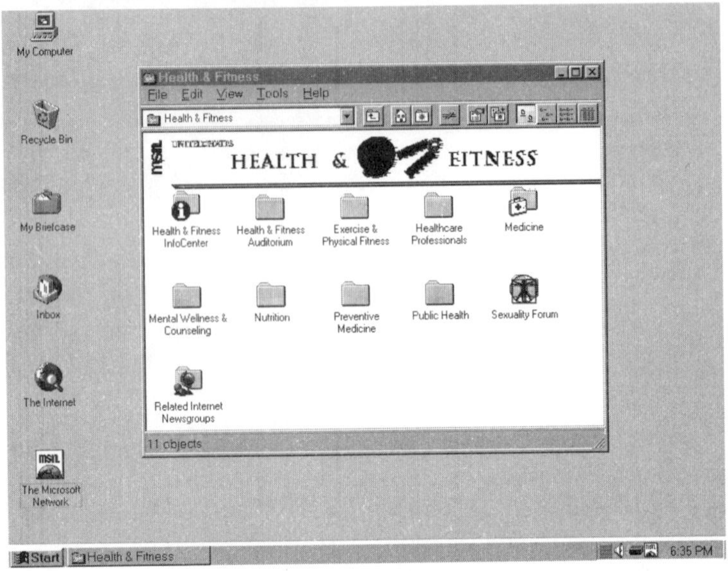

Figure 13.1 *The Health & Fitness category has forums of interest to anyone involved in their own or other's health.*

as the ones from NordicTrack. Many of the equipment manufacturers discussed here are present—if not on a regular basis, then for special events, to answer questions and give advice on their products.

When you are in touch with others using the same equipment you may find yourself more motivated to use it, and less likely to fall into the trap of paying thousands of dollars for exercise equipment only to have it sit idle. The same holds true for health club memberships. There is a lot of enthusiasm here, take advantage of it! After perusing this bulletin board you may become so eager to start that it's tempting to pick up the phone and order some hardware, but you may want to keep reading to see if you can find a bargain on something used from someone who is trading up.

For you body builders there is a forum all your own. To further your learning about body building, there are recommended reading lists and suggested television shows that are helpful. For the really serious there is a special bulletin board on the use and dangers of steroids. Whether you agree with their use or not, this bulletin board is extremely provocative, with strong feelings expressed on both sides of the issue.

But not all body building is that serious. If you use weights just to tone up, there is plenty of room for you here—not everyone wants to look like Mr. or Ms. Olympia. The chat rooms and bulletin boards here are for asking questions to ensure that any weight training you do will get you only the look you want. How many reps? How much weight? It can be confusing, and people are here to help.

Mental Wellness & Counseling

If a sound body makes for a sound mind, the reverse can be true as well. The near anonymity of on-line services such as MSN can be especially helpful when it comes to mental health. If you know of someone with a problem, check this area out. There are bulletin boards and chat rooms devoted to family counseling, eating disorders, stress disorders, and drug and alcohol abuse.

The support available in these forums is incredible. People are truly helpful. And best of all, they are always there when they are needed: at four in the morning, or at two in the afternoon. Not just once or twice a week across town, but at any time and in any place where there is a computer, help can be at hand.

For survivors of cancer, personal trauma, alcoholism, and other illnesses and traumas, there is a separate forum. The Survivors forum has regularly scheduled chats, along with on-the-fly ones. There are survival tips and a library of resources. If the concern is living with a long-term illness, there is a separate forum for that.

Medicine

Because of its very nature, the Medicine forum is an interesting mix. There are forums that are devoted to specialties such as pediatrics and oncology, to alternative medicine including acupuncture and herbal remedies, to medical equipment and new technologies, and to explosive, emotionally-charged issues such as abortion. What makes the mix so interesting is that we're all personally affected by medicine (unlike other professions) because we all have bodies that at some point need healing.

The bulletin boards in these forums contain messages from both professional and laymen alike. Frequently you'll find someone appealing to the on-line world to help diagnose an illness (this is *not* a substitute for a visit to a doctor!) or to clarify a health issue seen on television. Responses come from both groups, usually leading to further discussion.

The Nursing Network is a place for nurses to gather. As a profession, nursing can be both exhilarating and arduous, both physically and mentally. Here a nurse can share thoughts about the clinical, ethical, and psychological aspects of nursing with others who understand the many dilemmas. The forum also has discussion areas to cover the more mundane topics, such as political and legal issues. There is also helpful information on media resources, conferences, and education.

Preventative Medicine

Of course it would be better if we never got sick in the first place. In the Preventative Medicine forum you can share information about what works for you and get tips from others. As in the Medicine forum, participants include doctors, nurses, and just plain folks.

For a new age overview visit the Holistic Health forum (Figure 13.2). Here is a really wide range of holistic forums including movement therapy, energy techniques, massage,

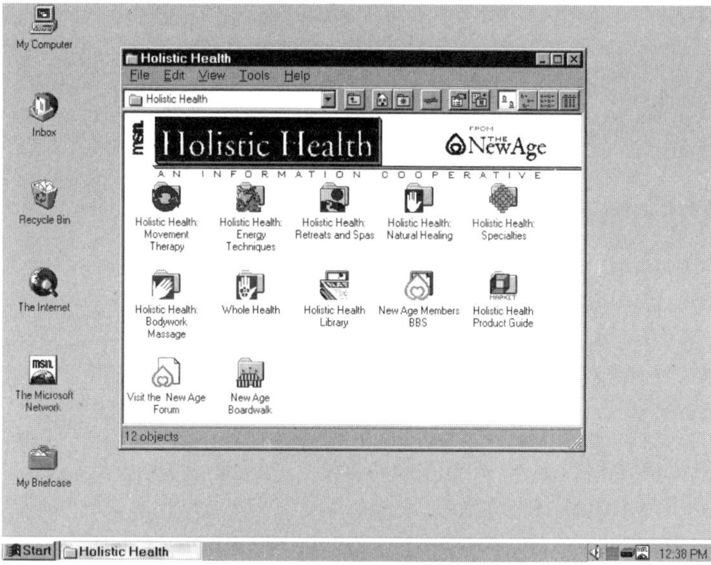

Figure 13.2 *The Holistic Health forum is a center for some alternative approaches.*

natural healing, and other specialties. There are product guides and guides to retreats and spas. And to help you make sense of it all, visit the Holistic Health Library.

Nutrition

Separate from, but related to the Preventative Medicine forum is the Nutrition forum. There are bulletin boards devoted to not only different foods and food groups but to vitamins, minerals, and supplements. Here you'll find discussions on nutrition and how it relates to disease, with special areas for pediatric, sports, adolescent, adult, and geriatric nutrition as well as a special area for nutrition and pregnancy. These forums are for the professional and layman alike.

To keep things lively, well known and some not so well known chefs and food and wine writers are frequent contributors. They serve up nutritionally responsible recipes and articles dealing with the different aspects of nutrition. Along with these there are interviews, chats, and other discussions plus a wide variety of products and services are for sale.

Public Health

There are many health issues that affect more than just the individual and extend to the society at large. In this category are subjects such as health insurance, socialized medicine, and rehabilitation and its associated costs in money and resources. Some diseases such as AIDS, cancer, and heart disease affect such a large number of people that they affect us all. These are the types of issues that the Public Health forums deal with.

Aside from the real problems above, another aspect of health that affects us all is misinformation. Misinformation can be rumors or just plain fraud. The Public Health forum has two misinformation forums, one for reporting misinformation and asking questions about what *appears* to be out there, and one for setting the record straight. Keeping an eye out for misinformation helps us all.

Sexuality

Like other areas in the Health & Fitness category, sexuality is one where you may prefer the anonymous nature of online conversation. Conversations here can be serious or fun, but to many they are embarrassing.

Much of the material here is not available for those under 18 years of age. To have access to all the forums you must register as an adult and request access to all newsgroups. To do this, open the Sexuality forum, and go to the Read Me First FAQ (frequently asked questions) folder.

The bulletin boards are not pornographic, but they can be sexually explicit. If you are offended by sexually explicit material, this is not the place to be. There are guidelines here for posting material to the bulletin boards. No flames (attacks on a person for his or her beliefs) or postings with really crude material are allowed, and under no circumstances can you post your personal phone number or address (if you have a sexuality-related business, that information can be made available).

General sexuality chat rooms and bulletin boards are found, as well as special forums for men and women, sex and the single person, survival guides for victims of sexual abuse, and how the twin issues of divorce and remarrying can affect sexuality.

After all the rules and regs, serious or not, you'll find a "Have Fun!" message. Do so with this and all the other categories as well!

CHAPTER 14

Home & Family

The Home & Family category (Figure 14.1) is really for anybody with a home or family, and I guess that includes all of us at one point or another. There are special forums for parents, for teenagers, and for kids as well as lots of areas for all, like vacation spots and forums on gardening, cooking, and other types of family recreation. There's often something going on in the Town Hall, where there is a set of chat rooms for special events and guest speakers.

Family Interests & Recreation

In this information age with us all plugged into the information superhighway or off pursuing individual interests, it is especially important to plan family activities. MSN makes this a fun and easy task. In the Family Interests & Recreation forum (and others as well) you'll find places to visit and things to do.

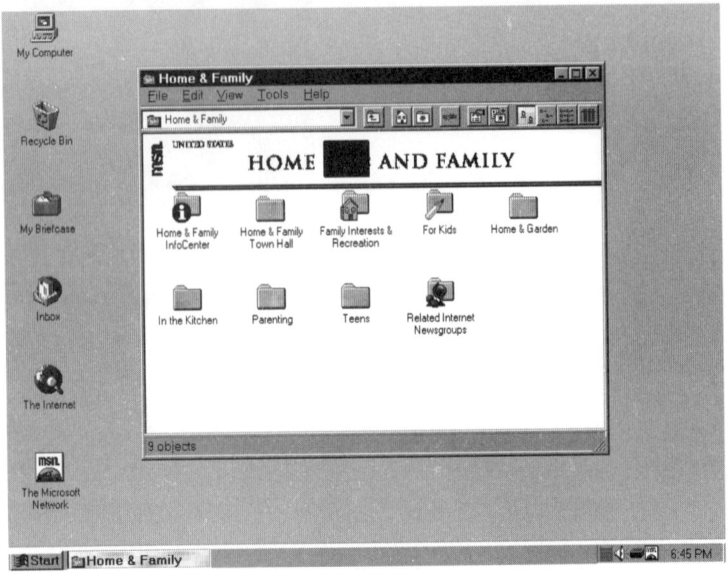

Figure 14.1 *The Home & Family category has forums for every member of the family.*

The Theme Parks! forum has detailed information on the world's major theme parks. Included are up-to-date hours and pricing both for lodging and meals. Other travel forums provide detailed information on small and large hotels, family resorts, all-suite hotels, and vacation spots where a condominium can be rented by the week. Constantly updated travel specials are posted, and to make sure that your stay will be as wonderful as you hoped, take some time on the bulletin boards and in the chat rooms to talk about your plans. Some places, such as Disney World, need their own set of tips and tricks for getting around to make the most of your hard-earned vacation. With other types of travel plans, you'll find that the tips about traveling with the whole gang are really helpful. Hear from others who have made a similar trip what can make the difference between a really enjoyable vacation and one you'd just as soon forget.

Other family interest forums include the Genealogy forum where you can search for unknown or long lost relatives around the world. The whole family can get involved, making up charts to map out the family tree. If you start getting somewhere, invest in some genealogy software to help keep track of it all. You'll find experienced speakers, product reviews, and recommendations to help.

When we're speaking of family, let's not forget Fido! Or Fluffy or Tweeter either. The Pets forum has chat rooms and bulletin boards for just about any critter in your family. Dogs, cats, fish, birds, reptiles, and small furry animals like rabbits and gerbils. For both the first-time pet owner with a hundred questions and for the more experienced one, there are tips on care and feeding and bulletin boards on special breeds. To really show off, send a favorite picture to the Photo and File Library. For more general conversations, visit the Pets General BBS & Chat forum.

Sports

Gone are the days when youth sports consisted of stickball on the corner or a lazy game of softball in the summer—now things are a little more complicated. In the Youth Sports forum you'll find helpful areas of special interest concerning all sports. Forums for the sport itself can be found in the Sports & Recreation category.

Here are forums for coaches, forums for asking questions of coaches, and bulletin boards for referees and players. If you are an organization such as a Little League chapter or part of a Parks and Recreation department, check out the Front Office. Whether you are an organization, parent or player, you're sure to need the helpful information in the Fundrai$ers bulletin board. Finally, for the talented or for that extra vacation time, look into the Camps, Exchanges, and Tournaments folder.

When you find an activity that the family enjoys, purchase the tools and toys you need on-line. There are catalogues for on-line shopping for products to help enhance the family recreation experience.

The Family Interests & Recreation forums described above are not the only forums in this area, which includes other topics that have been discussed elsewhere. For example, reading and photography are here and are also in the Arts & Entertainment category.

Kids

Computers are especially intriguing to kids, and MSN does not forget them. Spread across the Microsoft Network there are forums suitable for and enjoyable to children. Here there are club house chats and areas devoted to forming international Pen Pal relationships. Look up the neat stuff in the Science Fair forum and check out all the things that the ICPs have developed for kids on MSN, such as multimedia dailies, contests, and games. Children can easily get started in the Introduce Yourself bulletin board, describing themselves and their family. Children (or anyone else for that matter) should never post their home phone number or address! More about this in the Teens area, below.

Home & Garden

The Home & Garden forum is a multifaceted collection. It has financial information to assist in tracking your personal assets, buying a home, or improving an existing one.

It also has a Building a House forum and a Home Improvement bulletin board, with a special forum dedicated to designing children's spaces. And so you can really see what's going on there is a Home & Garden Multimedia forum.

Gardening has its own forum with its own bulletin boards and chat rooms. There are reference areas arranged alphabetically, a Gardening for Kids forum, and a place to Introduce Your Garden. Be proud of all that hard work, upload a picture!

In the Kitchen

More than just a recipe collection, In the Kitchen is where you'll find forums on all aspects of what goes into your body. Visit the Ale & Lager forum for information on brewing your own and on dining with beer. While you're here don't forget the Wine, Beer, Spirits & Cigars forum. You'll find bulletin boards and chats devoted to all four topics and a forum on winery tours—a wonderful tour to take while on vacation or to enjoy on any sunny afternoon.

But of course we can't exist on just wine, beer, spirits, and cigars! Take some time with the What's Cooking... Online forum. Have you ever tried a new recipe that looked good, only to find out it was awful? Now you can talk to the people who post the recipes. They've posted them because they've tried them and loved the results.

In the Recipes forum the recipes are of a general interest and categorized according to type (appetizer, dessert, salad, and so on) and main ingredient (eggs, fish, and poultry, for example) There are separate forums for Vegetarians and for those cooks (count me in here!) who are looking for Fast and Easy. And for the fervent lover of chocolate or the chili pepper freak, look at the recipes in the Passions forum.

Last, if food is your thing, remember to take a look at the Kitchen Table Talk forum. The numerous bulletin boards cover such diverse topics as restaurant and cookbook reviews, dieting, kitchen tips and hints, recipe management software, coupon-ing, and wine information and wine-making recipes.

Parenting

Very few things in life are as difficult, time-consuming, and taxing as bringing up children to be happy and productive citizens. The Parenting forum on MSN is full of friendly advice from other members and professionals alike. User bulletin boards cover topics as they come up that are familiar to all parents: how are others handling the allowance question, problems in school, or poor or destructive eating habits. You'll find a broad audience for all of your parenting questions, and what worked for other parents may work for you.

The Parenting in the 90s folder contains useful forums, chats, and bulletin boards on family entertainment, parenting special children, help when parents are divorced or separated, and help with the adopted child. Start off on the Introduce Yourself bulletin board. It's a great way to meet people. Tell a little about yourself, your children and their ages, and read about others. You'll soon find yourself in conversations with others in similar circumstances.

Also in Parenting is the Work at Home Dads forum for those men who have elected to stay at home to work and/or care for their children. There are newsletters, cookbooks, programs to download, and a place to upload pictures of the family. Not to be left out, here you'll also find a bulletin board for wives of stay at home dads! Working mothers have their own trials and tribulations—and forum. Talk to others in your position and get special help dealing with the child care and day care monster. The Children First! forum is for those who want expert advice and opinion from those who advocate that, in order for our society to function properly, children's needs must be addressed.

Teens

Teenagers have their own place on MSN with their own bulletin boards and chat rooms to meet other teens. For ages 13 through 18 and college age too, this forum is designed to be a place to just hang out and party a little bit. Post ideas and upload and download photographs, art, stories, and just neat files like games, utilities, wallpaper, and whatever. There are forums for debating the issues that concern teenagers today. There are separate forums to introduce other MSN sites of interest to teenagers and even a special forum to announce a birthday and have a party!

For Parents

Although this is not a separate category area in the Home & Family forum but only a forum in the Teen area, it deserves special mention. Please, please read the Please Read! Letter to the Parents. This letter contains invaluable information to keep your children safe and happy on-line. Although there are rules that must be adhered to, in a forum for preteens or teens there is a wide age-range, and what may be appropriate for the 19-year-old may not be appropriate for the 12-year-old! The Teen forum manager is available by appointment for a private chat and is of course available by E-Mail to answer any questions or to address any concerns. The main point is to be aware of what your children are doing on-line, who they are talking to, and what about. Parents need to teach their children the ropes, and they'll find tips and procedures here to do just that.

Home & Family Media

The word media can cover a broad range. This forum introduces family-oriented software, on-line publications, and Internet sites.

CHAPTER 15

Interests, Leisure, & Hobbies

If you've ever become involved in a hobby like stamp collecting or magic, you know what it is like to seek out people who share your fascination with the subject and can talk about it for hours. The trouble was you had to either go to a store (where you could only hang out for so long) or find a convention or specialty show. These are often far away or take place at an inconvenient time. Joining on-line clubs and visiting chat rooms or special events auditoriums can help fill that need.

Many of the forums seen here (Figure 15.1) appear in other categories with which they are closely aligned, and many you might expect to find here are elsewhere. As they say, if you don't see what you want, don't hesitate to ask! (Or use the Find function.)

Arts & Crafts

The Arts & Crafts forums are as diverse as the arts and crafts themselves tend to be. There are areas devoted to textiles, doll and stuffed-bear making, photography,

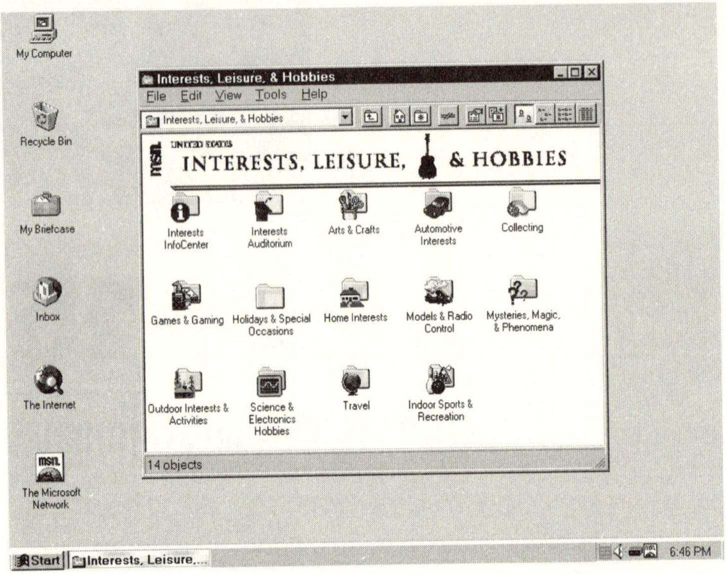

Figure 15.1 *The Interests, Leisure, & Hobbies category has forums for every taste.*

woodworking, pottery, sculpture, painting, and sewing. Each one of these is in turn broken down further. For example, look at Stitch, the sewing forum. Inside are forums for quilting, sewing, embroidery, and other needle arts.

If you sell what you create, visit the Crafters Marketplace to find out what's going on in your area of expertise.

Automotive Interests

Cars, light trucks, or motorcycles—this is the place! Whether you're looking to purchase a new or used vehicle or repair and maintain the one you have, you will find an authoritative source here. There are specialty areas for performance cars, classic and antique cars, trucks, 4x4's and off-road vehicles. You'll find classified ads and repair areas for all makes and models as well as a general discussion area. This is an area for everyone, not just car or motorcycle enthusiasts!

Collecting

As many different types of items as there are in the world, it seems that there are people to collect them. Artwork, antiques, memorabilia, stamps, coins, trading cards, even rocks and comic books—the comic books your mom threw out years ago that are worth a fortune now! There are forums moderated by MSN members and ICPs to give a distinct mix.

Collectors Direct (Figure 15.2) has forums for an incredible range of collecting topics, with scheduled and unscheduled chats, celebrity chats in different specialties, bulletin boards, manufacturer forums for talk about new products, on-line magazines, and complete services for shopping on-line, including current prices.

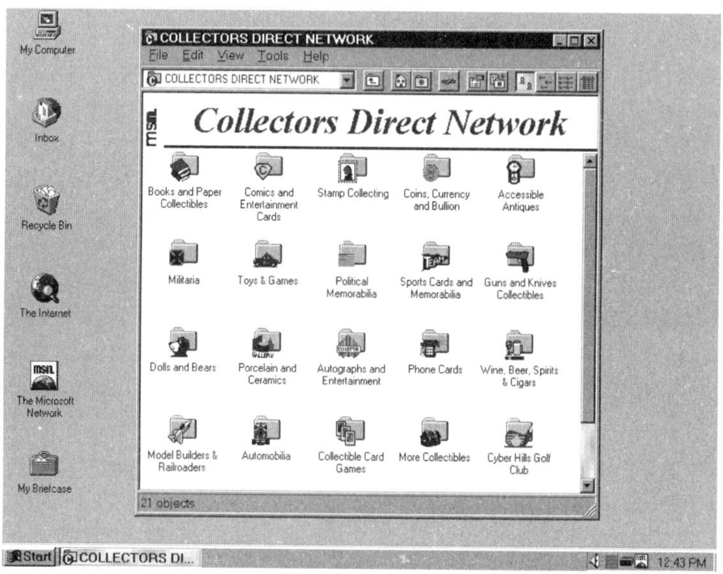

Figure 15.2 *Collector's Direct forum is for collectors of a variety of collectibles.*

Games & Gaming

The Games forums on-line are not limited to computer games, but rather include all games. There are traditional games like chess, modern trivia games, and on-line fantasy and strategy games. Computer games, role-playing games, video games, and collectible card games have their own forums, with chat rooms and bulletin boards. Many manufacturers are represented here with hints and advice. If you don't see your favorite game here, contact the forum manager. They are open to suggestions and if they receive enough requests, a forum will be born.

Holidays & Special Occasions

Who doesn't like holidays and special occasions? The forums here are on gift-giving, parties, and hosting special events. There are forums for exchanging ideas and forums for creating cards of your own on-line. American Greetings has an on-line presence where you can not only create your own cards, but spruce up your E-Mail as well. The company's bulletin boards are full of files with specialized icons and art work that is yours for a fee. Download it once and it's yours.

Home Interests

If you've checked out the Home & Family category you'll be familiar with the forums here. There are forums to benefit the entire family, such as the Food, Spirits, and Cooking forum, and the Pets forum. For those seeking to learn more about their family, look into the Genealogy forum. And for those trying to improve the family lot, there's a lot to be learned in the Gardening forums. If nothing grabs you at first glance, the Home Interests Internet Picks folder is full of related newsgroups.

Models & Remote Control

This forum is devoted not just to model building, but to the serious hobbyist. Whether you're into radio-controlled boats, helicopters, planes, or blimps, whether powered by electricity or gas, you'll find like-minded aficionados here. The space age is not left out, so check out the forums on Rocket Models and Space/Sci Fi Models.

Things don't stop with those flying machines though. Forums on car models and slot car racing, model railroading and radio-controlled boats, ships, and trucks abound. For those with an interest in matters military, there is a Military Models forum.

Tying it all together is the Announcements & Events forum, the Models & RC Chat, and the Model & RC File Library.

Mysteries, Magic, & Phenomena

Who among us doesn't have some interest in that which we don't understand? It's hard to resist exploring the unexplainable. Not that your questions will necessarily be answered, but whether it's checking your horoscope in the daily paper (Hey, you never know) to wondering about that thump in the night, you'll find like-minded people with whom to explore the unknown.

Astrology

The Astrology forum is all-encompassing. Begin by checking your chart and move on from there. Find out the compatibility of friends and lovers, read about financial astrology, and get help in picking times and dates that are good for you. For the more sophisticated, learn new astrological techniques and more about cycles and sciences and find out how computers are changing the field.

To keep current, look up the astrology magazines, the library, and the various astrology organizations, each of which has its own forum. Last, visit the Astrology Product

Guide for information on astrology software, learning astrology, and other astrology on-line services.

Alien Encounters and UFOs

Whether you've had alien encounters yourself (if you have and would like to report them, there's a spot for that here) or are just interested in the subject, there's lots here to get involved in.

There are forums on aliens in antiquity and historic UFO events. If the past is not what interests you, investigate the Current Alien Phenomena folder and the Future Prospects forum for a peek at what's coming.

Magic & Illusions

Everyone loves a magician. There's something about the willingness to suspend belief, even if only for a short time—how *did* that rabbit get into the hat? Perhaps it's because so many of us were introduced to magic as children that we continue to be fascinated by it as adults.

The Magic & Illusions forum has something for everyone. For the aspiring magician or those wanting to hone their skills there is the Magic School with its own class/chat room, library, magazines, and magic books bulletin board. And don't forget to review the Magic Trick of the Month!

There are calendars, fan clubs, and chat rooms for both special events and private chats. Performers will find special forums on juggling and balloon sculpture. And because seeing is believing (hah!), take a look at the Magic Photo & Video Gallery and send in your own to be included.

Points Beyond: Divination and Oracles

For those looking for other answers, or other mysteries, they may be found here. Among the areas are Tarot Card reading, the I Ching, runes, palmistry, and numerology. Each has its own forum with tips on the subject and any tools that may be of help.

Outdoor Interests & Activities

Like the Home Interests forums, this area has its own forums, but also encompasses many others from other categories. For example, the Astronomy & Space forum, dedicated to stargazing and space exploration, is by definition an outdoor activity, but also appears in the Science & Technology area. The areas in Outdoor Sports & Recreation are of course outdoor activities, but they were originally in the Sports & Recreation category, and so are covered there.

Flying

Whether you are a pilot or just interested in aviation, whether you are a seasoned pilot or a student, whether you own your own plane or are building one, this is the place to be. In addition to general aviation, there are bulletin boards on instruments, students and instructors, navigation and ATC, commercial aviation and military aviation. Related subjects are covered in bulletin boards for ownership issues, antiques and classics, and homebuilts, and is a forum on alternative aviation for soaring planes, gliders, balloons, and the like.

If you're going to be traveling, stop in at the Airshows & Museums bulletin board. And last, let's not forget in this computer environment, a special Flight Simulation bulletin board.

Because all the flying and aviation-related topics cover so much ground, from weather to physics, all the forums could not possibly be in one area. There are links to related sites on MSN and on the Internet.

Bird Watching

Speaking of flying, one of the more leisurely outdoor activities can be bird watching. Meet with others who share the passion and excitement of unexpected sightings and pass on your own. With a national and international network of devoted professionals and amateurs, tracking our flying friends will be that much more rewarding.

Science & Electronics Hobbies

The main points of interest here are the bulletin boards for Consumer Electronics and Electronics and the Amateur Radio forum.

Electronics

The Consumer Electronics bulletin board has the wider appeal, as we all have some interest in the electronic devices in our home. Topics include VCRs, home theaters, home and car stereo, televisions, telephones—in short, any personal electronics.

If you just like to keep up on the latest and the greatest, you will find people who share your enthusiasm. But the real benefit is when it is time to buy. Many of these items are not inexpensive, and the feedback that you get from other members is invaluable.

The Electronics bulletin board is for those who are interested in the actual electronics. There are discussions of schematics, circuit simulation, amplification, and the like.

Amateur Radio Forum

Amateur radio, better known as ham radio, has been around a long time. People were using it to communicate all over the world long before there were chat rooms. Topics here include HF, packet radio, scanners, satellite, and amateur TV. There is information on Swap meets and a file library for uploading and downloading files.

Travel

Even if you never get out of the house (or away from the computer) armchair travel is better than none. And if you do actually leave the premises, the information here will make your trip go more smoothly and be more enjoyable.

In the Travel forum are areas to put you in touch with other members interested in travel. There are chat rooms and bulletin boards for both the international traveler and those who are staying stateside. If you are interested in swapping homes instead of staying in more commercial lodgings, look at the Vacation Homes Exchanges bulletin board.

Independent content providers here include airlines and travel guides. You can purchase an airline ticket directly, check seating arrangements and make sure your frequent flyer mileage is kept up to date.

Check the special travel guides that are now on-line. Unlike guide books you purchase in the store, these are updated regularly and so are rarely incorrect because of being out of date.

Indoor Sports & Recreation

You'd never know how many things there are to do on a rainy day until you check out the Indoor Sports & Recreation forum. There are bulletin boards and forums for every conceivable indoor activity: billiards, which is enjoying a renaissance of sorts, body building, bowling, and boxing are just a start. If more physical movement is more your idea of recreation, then take a look at the Gymnastics, Recreational Dance, and Wrestling bulletin boards. Don't forget to check in at the Martial Arts Network and chat with Grand Master, get news of upcoming tournaments, and purchase uniforms, videos, and so on.

CHAPTER 16

News & Weather

It was not that long ago that most people eagerly opened the morning newspaper to read about the previous days events. Then, along came radio and television news. They'd listen to the car radio on the way home and catch up further with the evening news on television. Finally, along came on-line services, with their all-day news updates accessed from any computer, often from the office desk. Well, things have come full circle. Looking at the screen in Figure 16.1, you'll see some familiar names and faces.

MSN News

MSN News really does bring the front page to your desktop, with a difference. In addition to the print stories and photographs you would expect to find, there are video clips and sound clips. MSN News takes full advantage of Windows 95 and MSN technology. If you are reading a story about the Rolling Stones latest concert tour, there will be icons labeled Stones Fan Club bulletin board and chat room. Double-clicking will take you right there.

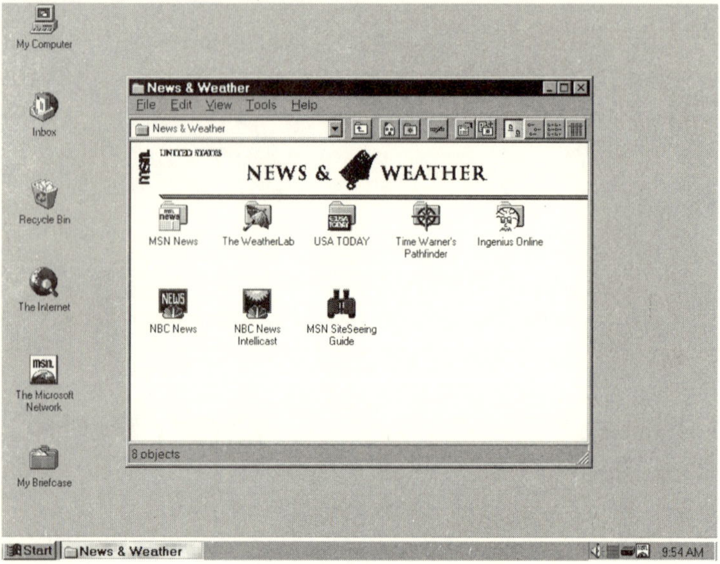

Figure 16.1 *The News & Weather category contains up-to-the-minute news, weather, and sports information from a variety of sources.*

The first time you open MSN news, the wait will seem interminable. Have patience. For one time only some necessary files are downloaded to your computer, and after that the wait will not be as long. Depending on your hardware, it may still seem pretty long though.

You can use your mouse to navigate along the screen to where you want to go, or click the MSN Browse button to get right to the page or story you are looking for. Then copy or print the page of the news that is of interest to you to be read later.

Access to some of the news sources on MSN, like USA Today and Time/Warner Pathfinder, requires that you have the Internet Explorer software installed. Other sources, like NBC News, work just fine with the baseline version of MSN.

USA Today

USA Today on-line is rather like having the Sunday papers everyday. Unlike the usual daily newspaper that has only a few sections, things are a lot easier to find with *USA Today*'s many different sections, or in this case, forums.

USA Today Front Page has the big stories of the day, while USA Today News has in depth coverage of other events. For financial matters turn to USA Today Money, and for lighter issues there is USA Today Life and the USA Today Crossword Puzzle (the puzzle can be set for different skill levels). You'll find complete sports coverage in USA Today Sports with up-to-the-minute scores in USA Today Real Time Scores. And because everybody's always talking about it, national and international weather reports are in the USA Today Weather.

NBC News & NBC Intellicast

NBC News is a full-fledged news viewer much like the MSN News viewer. Click on the different areas to get more in-depth coverage of a story. You'll also find hot buttons in the text on the top and bottom borders of the page to move you to other topics in the NBC area. You'll find not only the events of the day as you would expect in a news daily, but also features on the various television news personalities. NBC News Intellicast is an all-inclusive weather service.

Time Warner Pathfinder

Tine Warner's offering is based on the World-Wide Web and provides not only access to their leading magazines, such as *Time* and *Fortune*, but also the opportunity to interact with their editors, post messages on their BBS, and chat with other readers. It's often pointed to as an example of a very well designed web page, so by all means drop by if you have the Internet Explorer installed.

The WeatherLab

The WeatherLab is a wonderful forum for the person who is interested in the art and science of forecasting the weather. There are forecasts for over 600 United States and international cities, updated regularly, with detailed weather maps for all continents. For even more information there are satellite and radar images, along with maps of things like airport delays.

The weather enthusiast can ask questions of a meteorologist and get involved in weather chats and bulletin boards.

This Just In!

Many of the services described here are like your morning newspaper. They may be more interesting, lively, or fun, but they are still updated daily. There are ways to get even more current information. The *This Just In!* folder is a collection of read-only bulletin boards, each devoted to a specific topic or news category, each updated at least hourly. Bear in mind that they are not as slick as viewers such as MSN—there are no icons, video or audio clips, or fancy pictures, but they sure are timely.

iNews

With all this information now at your fingertips, information overload may be a real problem. The news may be updated in a timely fashion, but if you have to spend three days finding what you need to know, it will not do you much good. Now, any MSN subscriber can set up a personal filter reflecting his or her own business and personal interests. Once this is done iNews, from Individual Inc., will cull all pertinent items from numerous news sources, on specific topics, on a daily basis.

CHAPTER 17

People & Communities

All of the categories on MSN have ample room for people to reach out to one another. But People & Communities (Figure 17.1) takes this a step further. The entire purpose of the forums here is reaching out.

Advice & Support

If you know of anyone in trouble or are just looking for some support for a personal problem, take a look here. There are bulletin boards for family counseling, eating disorders, stress and related disorders, and psychology.

Survivors of personal trauma and serious or chronic illness have their own forum. Also found here is a bulletin board for alcohol abuse, where the recovering alcoholic can find help not just one day at a time, but one hour or one minute at a time.

Women Online

Computers and women are not a traditional mix, but the Women Online forum will change that. This is a place not only dedicated to women's interests and issues, but a place to become comfortable with the Microsoft Network in a friendly atmosphere. Women can practice their on-line skills and ask questions that they might feel amateurish asking elsewhere. And because there are also topics of interest to women elsewhere on MSN, a special forum has been set up with links to them here.

Women's Wire

Women's Wire is a truly interactive publication. There are three main forums: Health & Fitness, Career & Finance, and Fashion & Shopping. In them you'll find child care tips that relate to both home and office, financial information with a focus on women, and personal information on topics such as exercising during pregnancy.

People to People

People to People is all about focusing on particular generational and interest groups. You'll find forums for seniors, people with disabilities, New Age followers, and the gay and lesbian community.

The DisAbilities Forum

This area on MSN is a support area dedicated to all people who are directly or indirectly affected by a disability. This could be the individual who is disabled, or a friend, co-worker, employer, or family member. Part of the support includes special events and unscheduled and regularly scheduled get togethers in Café Chat. There are bulletin boards on disability lifestyles, support, technology, and libraries.

Senior Net

Senior Net is a not-for-profit organization whose goal is to enrich the lives of older citizens (age 55 and up) via computer technology. The people at Senior Net have a lot of experience bringing computer technology into people's lives. In addition to Senior Net's on-line presence, it has 75 Learning Centers throughout the United States, holds national conferences, publishes a quarterly newsletter and its own instructional material, and offers discounts on software and other computer-related material.

To learn more about the organization and how to join, start off in the Membership Office to learn if you can benefit from membership, then start exploring. There are bulletin boards on computers as well as on finance and on public policy as it relates to seniors in society. The Pathways to Learning forum has shortcuts to the many computer courses available on MSN, and Senior Net has its own Software Libraries. These libraries are not just computer-related but cover travel, nutrition, and other subjects of interest available to the senior citizen community for uploading or downloading. For an even wider range, look up the What's HOT on the Web for Internet sites.

Planet Out

This forum focuses on the gay, lesbian, bisexual, and transgender groups. Although its primary language is English, it is an international site, with support for eight languages. Options shown now include Deutsch, English, Espanol, Francais, Italiano, Nederlands/Vlaams, Portuguese, and Russkaya. Japanese and Chinese will soon be on the list.

More than just an area for discussion groups, every effort is made to bring the best artistic efforts in writing, audio, photography, and the other arts from the community. There are special forums for health and fitness, legal issues, coming out, and religion and spirituality. For specific discussion areas on the different groups in the community, visit the Communities forum. For more general discussions and chats, go to the Civic Center.

New Age Forum

The New Age Forum is for those people looking for alternatives in life, and alternative answers to life's many questions. Forums include those for astrology, whole spirit, whole earth, whole food, whole person, and holistic health. The New Age Media forum contains books, magazines, cartoons and humor, libraries, and newsletters. And don't forget to check out the Market Place where there is an Organic Wine Shop, a New Age Art Gallery, Great Rugs, New Age Music, Classifieds, and a New Age Deli to offer everything else (everything except a pastrami on rye). Unfortunately, technology has not come *that* far!

Religion

The Religion forum is for everybody: those who need spiritual guidance, and those who offer it. The Religion forum contains bulletin boards for people of various faiths to establish an on-line sense of community, while the Religious Professionals & Organizations are for members of the clergy. For those who are concerned about how religion affects our every day lives, visit the Religion in Our World forum. Here there are discussions on religion in the news and media, religious entertainment, missions and outreach groups, and ethics and science. There are forums for religious philosophies and more general bulletin boards for sacred texts and religion files as well as a prayer exchange.

CHAPTER 18

Public Affairs

The Public Affairs category is a catch-all for forums for public services. Politics and politicians, government agencies, unions, public health, safety, and the media are subjects that are covered here (Figure 18.1).

Consumer Services & Information

The main focus here is consumer protection. Forums may contain general information, product information, and consumer guides.

Fire Service & EMS Forum

Health and fire safety are everyone's business. This forum is for all people who are concerned with fire and accident prevention. There are areas devoted to keeping the home safe and the office safe. Find out how to be safe outdoors by looking into Safe Outdoor Burning and Plants and Firesafe Landscaping. Children have an area of their own called Kid's Room where they learn what they can do to keep themselves safe and protect others. There are general

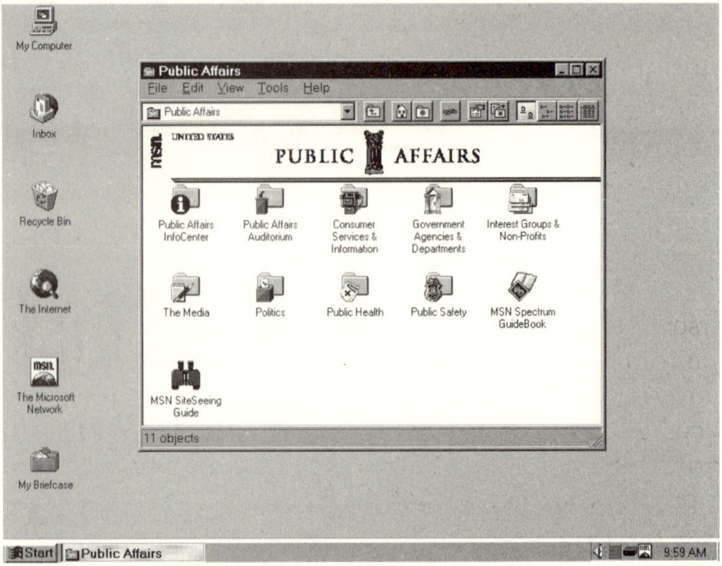

Figure 18.1 *The Public Affairs category has the tools to bring about the greater involvement of all citizens.*

information forums and a subscription-only forum for health and safety professional personnel.

Non-Line: Non-Profit Network

Non-profit organizations have special needs, from fund raising to keeping up with state and federal regulations. Here are forums on management techniques and funding information, with separate forums on Federal Domestic Assistance, Federal RFPs (Requests for Proposals), Points of Contact and Resources, and Nationwide Data and Information as well as a State by State guide. Youth Today magazine is for those concerned with legislation and funding issues and how they affect our nation's children.

The Applied Research & Development forum is an area dedicated to improving and making available existing resources for non-profits. Where necessary, they create new resources for helping organizations.

Government Agencies & Departments

This forum focuses on public services, management agencies, regulations, national security, foreign relations and trade, and really anything that pertains to our governmental agencies.

Armed Forces Forum

The Armed Forces forum is for all branches of the military, each with its own forum. There are forums for military personnel and for their families. For each there are forums on military support organizations, chat rooms and bulletin boards to introduce yourself, and ones for general discussion.

If you are interested in things military happening today (or perhaps tomorrow), check out the Wars & Rumors of Wars forum.

Interest Groups & Non-Profits

The forums here are focused on smaller groups with a shared interest in public affairs. There are forums for labor unions and corporate and special interest groups. Included here is Non-Line: Non Profit Network (discussed in Consumer Services and Information, above).

Policy Street: Public Policy

This is a forum devoted to public policy—how it affects us and how we can affect it. Topics include civil rights, defense, economics, education, environment, federalism, foreign affairs, health care, immigration, labor, political process, society and values, trade, tax, telecommunications, and welfare. There are Public Policy Organizations and Multimedia forums, an Events Calendar, and an on-line newsletter.

The Media forum covers all aspects of the media, including political publications and, in the Journalism forum, the effects of mass media. There are Job Market and Resources forums and bulletin boards for print, television, radio, and wired media. Other categories for discussion are high school journalism, campus journalism, crime and courthouse reporting, environmental journalism, and computer journalism.

On-line publications include *The American Spectator*, *The New Republic*, and *USA Today*.

Politics

For any political junkies out there, you've found your spot. There's coverage here of political campaigns and elections, with the politicians taking part. Find news on political issues and parties. For the more studious, there's a forum on political theory.

There are separate bulletin boards on national policy, foreign policy, economic policy, social policy, legal policy, political philosophy, and political reference, as well as a Political Reference File Library.

GoverNet: The Political Machine

With access to MSN, you have access to the political machine itself. Different branches of government have forums of their own. The White House forum has forums for the President and presidential wannabes, the Senate and the House both have forums available for each of their elected officials. There are State & Local Politics and Famous Speeches & Text bulletin boards. The Voter Alert forum lets you knows what bills are pending in Congress and gives you the means to immediately let your elected officials know how you feel about them, while the Congressional Report Card lets you know how they are doing.

Public Health

Public Health covers all areas of health that affect the general public. There are separate bulletin boards for AIDS, health insurance, rehabilitation, and socialized medicine as well as a general purpose bulletin board for health issues. This area is also covered in the Health & Fitness category.

Public Safety

All aspects of public safety have a place here. There are areas for law enforcement, fire and accident prevention, emergency services, private security services, home and personal safety, and gun laws.

Law Enforcement

The Law Enforcement forum is for both law enforcement personnel and those interested in law enforcement issues. There are bulletin boards and chat rooms, a suggestion box, and links to law enforcement newsgroups.

CHAPTER 19

Science & Technology

The Science & Technology category contains forums from every relevant discipline, with related chat rooms, bulletin boards, newsgroups, and file libraries (Figure 19.1). Unlike many other categories, there is a categorywide file library, as so many areas of science are interrelated.

Biology & Life Sciences

This forum currently contains bulletin boards dedicated to biology, ecology, and the environment, life sciences, and biomedical engineering. The Nursing Network is also located here (this was discussed in Chapter 13, covering the Health & Fitness category).

Chemistry

Here in the Chemistry forum you'll find bulletin boards in all areas including a general one and ones for environmental chemistry, health and chemistry, chemical engineering, and science and tech history. There are forums for the

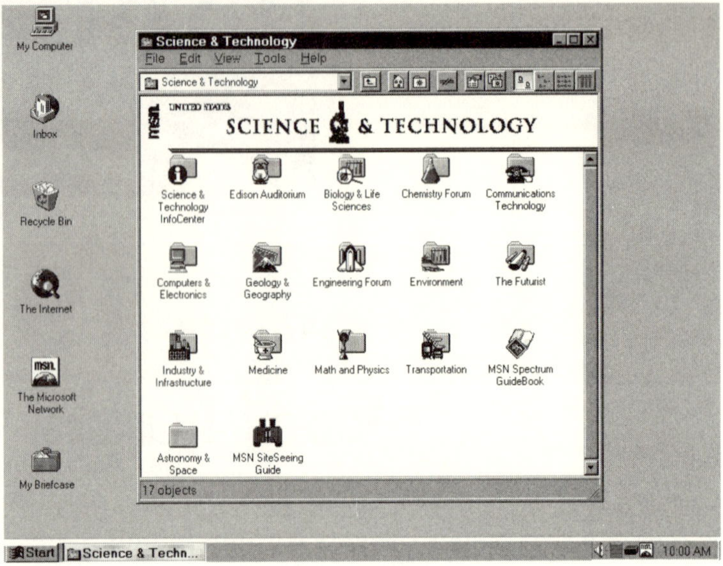

Figure 19.1 *The Science & Technology category.*

Journal of Chemical Education, on environment and health, and on chemistry software, with libraries, discussions, and reviews. For the student there is a Student Help Center.

Communications Technology

Since communication technology is what got us here, there are discussions covering all aspects and new developments in the communications field.

A look at the Communications Technologies bulletin board reveals titles on ISDN (integrated service digital network), ISDN versus frame relay, networking, modems, and cellular phones. Any topic that has anything to do with communications is fair game here.

The Mass Media bulletin board is for those interested in the technology of the mass media such as television and radio. Topics range from television operations and video conferencing to cable television, broadband connectivity, and connectivity in the home.

Amateur Radio Forum

The Amateur Radio forum is for all those HAM operators still with us. There are HAM chats (although since HAMs have been chatting over the radio for years internationally and locally, this may seem a little strange, even backward!) and a wide range of bulletin boards. In addition to a general interest one, there are ones on packet radio, short-wave radio, amateur radio, amateur television, satellite, and ARES/RACES, as well as an Amateur Radio File Library and an Amateur Radio Suggestion Box.

Computers & Electronics

The Computers & Electronics area is set up primarily as a discussion area for multimedia, networking, and other electronics technologies, including home electronics and a separate forum on robotics.

There are bulletin boards for computer networks, computer technologies, electronics, consumer electronics, and consumer electrical discussions.

Robotics

Anyone who remembers *The Cat in the Hat* by Dr. Seuss can appreciate what a robot can do! This forum is devoted to the exploration of robotics and electromechanical technology. It encompasses both industrial and hobby applications. There are forums for general robotics topics and for industrial robotics topics; for kids under 18 years of age there is Runsterbot.

The General Robotics forum has discussions on technology, medical robotics, Robo Aides for the handicapped, and animatronics for robots in film, including robotic animals and puppets. Buildbot is for those who build their own; Telepresence Teleoperation is for work robots that are used in handling hazardous substances or dangerous objects (such as bomb deactivation) and for space and water exploration. Then there's the Robot Law & Crimes bulletin board (just in case you get mugged by a robot) for all of us.

Industrial Robotics In addition to a forum for industry specific applications, here you'll find a general area with bulletin boards on input transducers, mechanical systems, power units, robotics mechanics, and system controllers. Bulletin boards for specific industries include those on semiconductor fabrication, food processing, metal welding, plastics fabrication, and machine tools machining.

Geology & Geography

The Geology & Geography forums cover not only geology and geography but meteorology and geophysics. Topics include planetary composition, landforms, and the geophysical laws. There are bulletin boards devoted to the earth sciences, geography and navigation, and geology, with a tie-in to USA Today Weather.

Engineering

One of the stated objectives of the Engineering forum is to make it accessible to everyone—engineering professionals, students, and enthusiasts—and in this it has been successful. A look at the forum (Figure 19.2) reveals a wide range of offerings, from the serious (Engineering Disciplines) to the amusing (Welcome Wave) to the helpful (Engineering Employment). The Events Calendar is updated regularly with news of upcoming special events, while the Chat Timetable has information on scheduled chats in Engineering Chat.

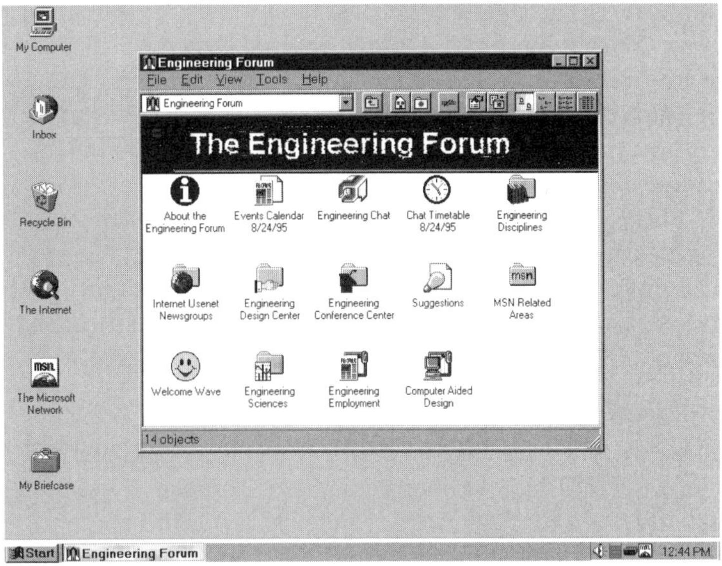

Figure 19.2 *Engineers have always tried to "push the envelope," and this area is no exception.*

Engineering Disciplines

For specific areas of interest and for a general interest Engineering bulletin board, this is the place. There are bulletin boards here for chemical engineering, civil engineering, computer aided design, environmental engineering, and mechanical engineering. There are also boards for naval and marine engineering, nuclear engineering, manufacturing and production engineering, software engineering, aerospace engineering, automotive engineering, and biomedical engineering. For the student there is the Engineering Students' Corner.

Engineering Design Center

The Engineering Design Center bills itself as a virtual design center. There is a Meeting Room, which is a chat room set aside to discuss projects and to hold meetings in, and a chat room called The Cafeteria for just hanging out and relaxing with other engineers. The Filing Cabinet bulletin board is for uploading technical papers and engineering articles. Project proposals are also welcome, along with reports to broaden the knowledge base of everyone in the engineering community.

The Engineering Design Center is also host to the Engineering Standards Library forum. Here you will find bulletin boards open for the posting of current engineering and design standards and prospective ones. Also included are bulletin boards for specific standards organizations.

Engineering Sciences

Here there are bulletin boards for each of the engineering sciences. Included are boards for structural and stress analysis, weights and mass properties, dynamics and vibrations, and materials science. There are also boards for thermo-dynamics, acoustics, aerodynamics, and fluids analysis.

If the particular science or engineering discipline you are looking for is not here when you log on, there is a download-and-run suggestion box. Just double-click the Suggestions icon, enter the information, and it will be transmitted to the appropriate party.

Environment

The forums here are devoted to our natural resources and how we handle them, the global warming effect, pollution and pollution control, and air and water quality.

Included are bulletin boards for environmental chemistry and ecology and the environment.

GNET Environment Technology

The GNET forum is for those people seeking business opportunities in the environmental area. Providing strategic market information, the Global Network for Environment & Technology was developed by the Global Environmental

Technology Enterprise (GETE) through a cooperative agreement with the Department of Energy. In addition to an Environment & Technology chat room, there are numerous forums, each with its own bulletin board and forums.

Publications

This area contains articles from many publications, including *Environmental Business International, Inc.*, that concentrate on environmental news and policy from a market perspective.

News & Events

This is a collection, updated weekly, of summaries of environmental articles gathered from over 750 sources. Previous week's summaries are kept on-line, available for review.

Environmental Technologies

New environmental technologies are emerging constantly. This area concentrates on technologies in all stages of development, including those available now and those firmly rooted in the future. There is a catalog of products available from a wide range of sources, including the federal government, academia, and commercial enterprises. These technologies are rated on a price/performance ratio with both technical and commercial applications and descriptions.

To help with the promotion of environmental technologies and their uses, described here are programs at the federal, state, and local levels.

Environmental Industry & Market

Potential business leads can be found in this environmental market forum. There is information on both the public and private markets for goods and services, and you may find help here and advice on requests for proposals (RFPs) and licensing as well as data on sites in need of remediation.

Market Intelligence forums include papers available for downloading on a variety of topics, including air pollution control equipment, solid waste management, water equipment and chemicals, remediation, environmental instrumentation, and exports and global market update.

Regulation, Law & Policy

Finally, this forum catalogues and provides summaries of all major environmental laws and policy as they pertain to the marketplace.

Earthwatch

Earthwatch, a non-profit organization, was founded in 1972. Its mission is to further the understanding, and to improve the quality, of life on our planet earth. More than 1,000 proposals are sent each year to Earthwatch and its affiliate, the Center for Field Research, from scholars in need of money and volunteers. Of these, approximately 150 projects are given the go-ahead each year.

There are several areas where everyone can get involved, including the Base Camp bulletin board for general discussions of Earthwatch projects, environmental issues, science, or anything that relates to Earthwatch's missions. The Project of the Week is a place where a current project is highlighted for one week with particularly unusual findings or special pricing information.

Mission Alerts

Dolphin intelligence, Kenya's wild forest, the wolves of India, and Costa Rican sea turtles are just some of the projects listed on this bulletin board. The idea here is to read about upcoming and ongoing projects and field research sites that need volunteers (that's you!). Information on assignments and accommodations for volunteers, the research and expedition's goals, and profiles of the principal investigator and staff are included.

Image Library

This bulletin board is for present and past staff members and volunteers to upload images of their Earthwatch projects.

The Futurist

Ah, but that we could all tell the future. Well there are those who, if not able to exactly predict the future, are trying to bring it about. In this forum are forums for those involved in discovering and harnessing new technologies, such as artificial intelligence (AI), and the self-anointed visionaries who write and dream about them.

21st Century Online

21st Century Online is an international network of entrepreneurs who are excited about what tomorrow brings. They are involved in software creation, writing, graphic design, and marketing techniques. In fact, they are involved in just about everything, but share the common thread of entrepreneurship and an eye toward the future.

There are conferences on doing business in cyberspace and how to take advantage of the amazing new opportunities on-line. For all entrepreneurs there is information from experts on business skills that only experience can bring. For example, there are specialized conferences with top futurists such as Alvin Toffler and Intel CEO Andy Grove. For the film-maker, there are interviews with stars, producers, directors, and writers working in the film industry; for the writer or lover of books, there are conferences and bulletin boards featuring authors from the *New York Times* best seller list.

Emerging Computer Technologies

Although it may seem that all computer technology is emerging, this forum focuses on the newer, less common ones. There are forums and/or bulletin boards devoted to artificial intelligence, virtual reality, voice recognition, and interactive television.There will be more, but since they have not yet emerged, we'll just have to wait!

This forum contains bulletin boards for general discussions and for specific topics, such as the hardware and software necessary for virtual reality applications.

Artificial Intelligence

AI has its own forum with a suggestion box, newsletters, file library, and Chat Center. The Chat Center has a chat room for scheduled chats and areas for chat archives. There is a Resource Corner with bulletin boards on professional associations, conferences and workshops, publication information, and employment opportunities. There are links to related areas on MSN and to related Internet newsgroups.

Industry & Infrastructure

This forum covers every aspect of our consumer society. There are forums on consumer goods and transportation and on power systems, construction, and manufacturing. Publications include the *Smithsonian Magazine* and *Air & Space Magazine* with attendant chat rooms and bulletin boards. You have the ability to subscribe to these on-line.

Medicine

The Medicine Forum is for all of those involved with modern medicine. There are areas for family practitioners, specialists, and nurses. Topics include alternative medicine areas such as acupuncture and controversial subjects such as abortion.

Healthcare Professions Forum

This is a forum for all professionals involved in healthcare. There is a regularly scheduled Healthcare Chat and a Healthcare BBS. Other bulletin boards include a Healthcare Software Library and a Healthcare Classified BBS for the posting of job opportunities, jobs wanted, equipment to sell, or any other healthcare-related ad. This is for individuals only, no agents!

For MDs, DOs, DDSs, DCs, DPMs, PHDs, and the rest, there is a lounge area with a chat room and bulletin board for the easy exchange of information. Those involved in critical care subspecialties have a separate forum with a lounge and bulletin boards for discussion, files, and suggestions. Nurses have their own forum: the Nursing Network Forum.

For those in the UK, visit the United Kingdom Healthcare forum. There are chat rooms, bulletin boards, and an Internet connection for issues specific to healthcare in the UK.

Math and Physics

This forum is dedicated to the discussion of the theories and applications of math and physics. Bulletin boards and chat rooms are for all disciplines from solid-state to cosmological physics and all aspects of mathematics, be it number theory or group algebras.

Transportation

Planes, trains, and automobiles! The Transportation forum is dedicated to these and more. In addition to a general Transportation bulletin board, there are boards for the discussion of aviation technology, automotive technology, marine technology, and mass transportation.

Astronomy & Space

Who among us hasn't gazed up into the sky to wonder? This forum is a gathering area for those who are interested in astronomy and space exploration. You'll find bulletin boards with NASA Press Releases, *Astro Magazine* with weekly articles from well known people in the field, and Astro Exchange for selling and swapping books and equipment. Both astronomy and space exploration have their own general bulletin board and file libraries for software, images, and text files. As an added bonus, there is a special bulletin board devoted to shuttle launches as they occur and updated with progress reports.

CHAPTER 20

Sports & Recreation

Whether you are an avid player or an avid spectator, there's a lot that the Sports & Recreation category can offer (Figure 20.1). The Victory Pavilion has information on special events with celebrity guests from the sports world, including athletes, reporters, managers, coaches and the like. For all sports you'll find daily results, standings, and statistics.

Field & Court Sports

The most popular games in America fit into this category. You'll find bulletin boards on baseball, football, and basketball (for the true basketball fan don't forget to check out ShaqWorld Online, Shaquille O'Neal's on-line forum!). There are also boards on soccer, hockey, volleyball, rugby, cricket, and lacrosse. A separate forum is devoted to racket sports such as tennis, racquetball, badminton, squash, and a general racquet sports board.

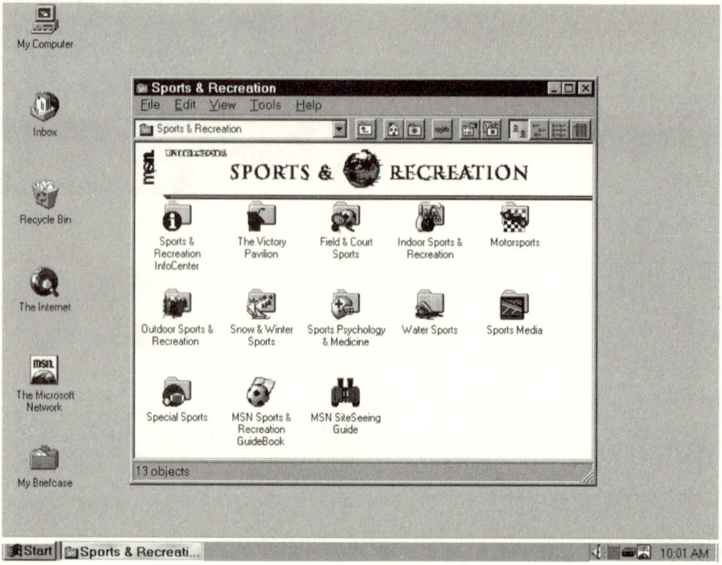

Figure 20.1 *The Sports & Recreation category has a full complement of both indoor and outdoor sports as well as other recreation forums.*

Indoor Sports & Recreation

Not all sports take place outside, of course. There's plenty happening indoors! A look at this forum reveals activities that can be quite physically taxing, as well as those that are not but may still require much skill.

In the former category are bulletin boards on boxing, gymnastics, and recreational dance. There are forums devoted to body building and weight training, the martial arts, and wrestling.

In the latter category are bowling and billiards—although, for all I know, they may give some a good workout! In any case, for everyone there is an Indoor Sports bulletin board and an Indoor Sports Chat.

Motorsports

This area deals with all aspects of racing including auto, motorcycle, marine, and airborne.

In addition to a general Motorsports bulletin board and chat room, each type of racing has its own forum. The Auto Sports forum includes bulletin boards on Formula 1, Indy, stock cars, 4-wheel and offroad, drag racing, rally racing, and a special forum for the British Grand Prix. Look into the other forums for their special interest boards, such as those on powerboats and different motorcycle events.

Outdoor Sports & Recreation

The Outdoor Sports & Recreation forum is particularly inclusive. It seems to contain bulletin boards and forums on every conceivable outdoor sports activity! Along with the usual general interest bulletin board and chat room, you'll find boards on camping, climbing, cycling, equestrian activities, and triathlons. Hiking, running, golf, and fishing each have their own forums.

The Hiking forum has areas devoted to pictures and maps, national parks, national forests, hiking equipment, and camp cooking. There's a paper on different clubs and organizations, and, if you'll be out for a while, be sure to take a look at the Wilderness Medicine forum.

The Fishing forum has bulletin boards each dedicated to different areas of fishing. Included are fresh water fishing, fly fishing, and salt water fishing. There are also boards for catalogs and reference materials, tournaments and events, and a file library.

For those interested in more extreme sports there is an Extreme Sports folder, with bulletin boards covering downhill skiing and snowboarding, skating and skateboarding, skydiving, surfing, whitewater sports, and bungee jumping. The Archery & Firearms forum includes information on archery, firearms, hunting, paintball, and skeet and target shooting.

Snow & Winter Sports

This area is for all sports that require cold or snow. Ice skating, skiing and snowboarding, sledding, and hockey are represented. The Skiing & Snowboarding forum has bulletin boards both for downhill skiing and snowboarding and for cross country skiing.

Sports Psychology & Sports Medicine

This area is for the discussion of the treatment of injuries in sports, their prevention, and the psychological aspects of injuries and competition. There are bulletin boards devoted to sports medicine and sports psychology.

Water Sports

Who can resist the allure of water sports on a hot summer day? Even just watching seems to cool one off. There are bulletin boards for rowing, wind surfing, surfing, swimming and skin diving, scuba diving (scuba divers also have a magazine, *Scuba On-line!*, in a separate forum), water skiing, canoeing and kayaking, whitewater sports, and power boating. Sailing has its own forum, with a bulletin board and chat room and a full complement of forums and information on the Americas Cup Race.

Sports Media

The Sports Media forum is a collection of all the sports-related media found on MSN (Figure 20.2). From the lesser-known Gold Sheet, which offers specialized information for the football and basketball betting crowd, to the well-known NBC Sports, the sports enthusiast will get a wonderful overview, including statistics, scores, and other up-to-date information on sporting events.

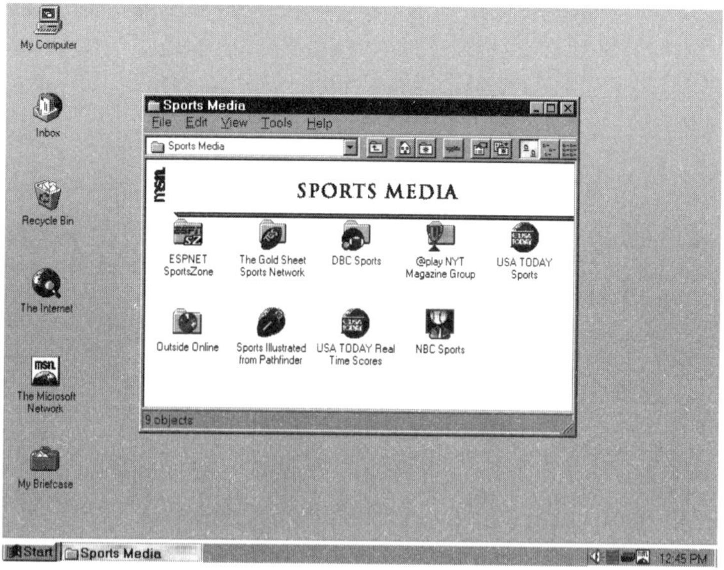

Figure 20.2 *The media represented on MSN are from both the print media world and new on-line undertakings.*

Special Sports

Whether it's wheelchair basketball, special skiing, or active participation in the Special Olympics, there's something here for everybody.

CHAPTER 21

Surfing the Internet with MSN

The Microsoft Network gives you several ways of exploring the Internet, a global network of interconnected computer resources. The Internet (a.k.a. the information superhighway, the infobahn, and many other hyperbolic names) is the largest computer system in the world. Finding just what you're looking for on it can be difficult and time consuming (or sometimes alluringly easy), but if it isn't there, either it doesn't exist in computer-transmittable form or you're looking on the wrong planet! If you have a plain-vanilla installation of MSN (without the Windows 95 Plus Pack), you can access the text-based Internet newsgroups and forums on MSN via the Internet Center, which can be found on the Categories main page. If you have the Plus Pack, the Internet Explorer provides easy access to the graphical and intuitive World-Wide Web.

Connecting from the Internet Center

Clicking on the Internet Center brings you to a page of additional choices, as shown in Figure 21.1, including forums discussing Internet access and libraries of useful utilities as well as the various Internet newsgroups themselves, which can be found by double-clicking on the Internet Newsgroups icon. The newsgroups are split into Usenet newsgroups, The Most Popular NewsGroups, Other Popular Newsgroups, and Regional and International Newsgroups, as shown in Figure 21.2. Usenet groups cover a wide range of topics, including computers, the natural sciences, news, social sciences, recreation, and a host of other subjects. The "most popular" category, at least according to Microsoft, includes a number of news boards, some job posting boards, some humor boards, and forums on Unix and programming in C. No arguing taste, I guess. The "other" group contains the bit, biz, bionet, and the

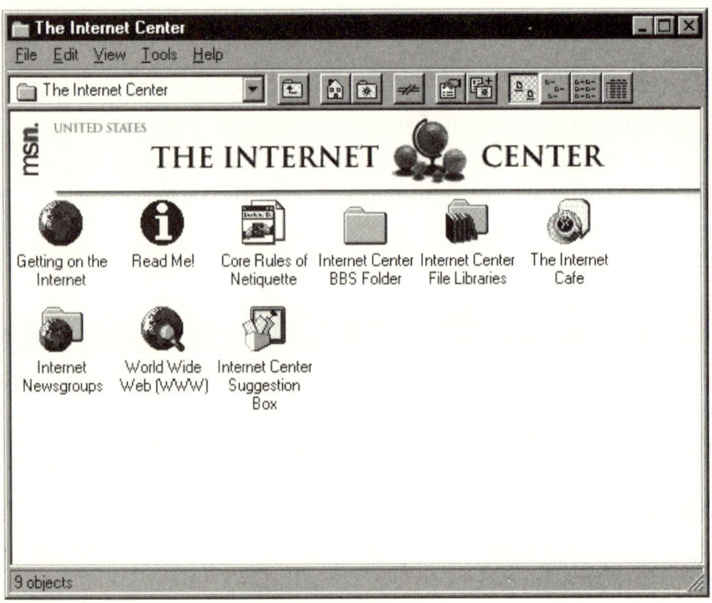

Figure 21.1 *The Internet Center, with its own forums and libraries, is a good place for both the Internet beginner and those with more experience.*

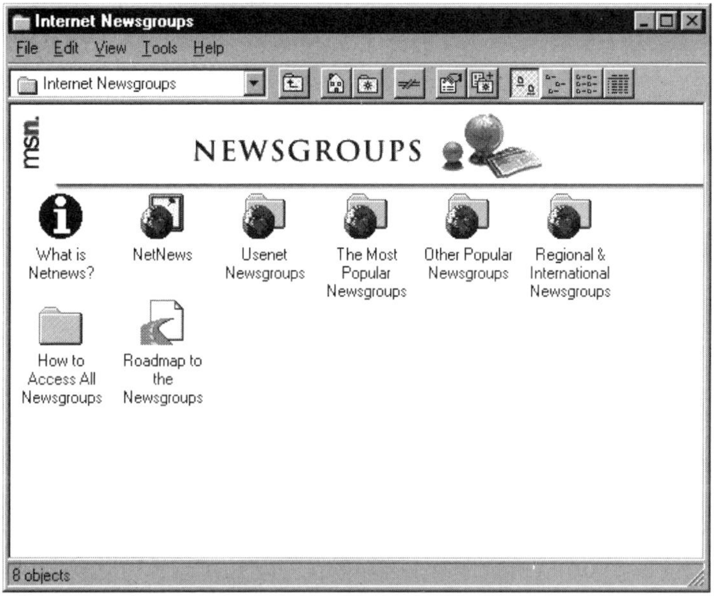

Figure 21.2 *Microsoft's selection of popular or regional and international newsgroups point you in the right direction.*

infamous alt newsgroups, all of which are uncensored and, generally, unmoderated. The regional groups include Europe as well as the 50 states of the U.S.

Like the forums on MSN, newsgroup postings are typically grouped into threads of articles on loosely related topics. To access the full range of uncensored Usenet groups, you'll need to fill out an electronic form (or *e-form,* in the parlance of Windows 95) verifying that you are over 18 years of age and actively desire access to material that some folks will find offensive.

The final release version of MSN does allow you to post your own contributions to the ongoing discussions. This is a decidedly mixed blessing—as you'll quickly see, the Internet community is decidedly less tolerant of "newbie" ignorance than are most commercial services. America Online members in particular seem to have developed a bad rep on the Internet for making entirely avoidable errors, and the acronym AOL is often used in a context that makes it clear that the A may stand for something much more scatological than "America." Now that MSN does allow posting, you'll find that it's a very good idea to read the FAQs and existing documents before blithely imposing on other people's bandwidth to ask who's buried in Grant's Tomb.

Areas that are intended to let newbies make their predictable errors before inviting the wrath of others are alt.test (which is intended to let people practice their posting technique free from the concern of annoying others by their faux pas) and alt.1d (one-dimensional graphics and the thought behind it—think about it), which until the advent of alt.0d was the first alt. newsgroup you'd see in an alphabetic list and thus a likely starting point/catch basin for giving something for newbies to cut their teeth on.

The least controlled of the Usenet groups are the alt. (for alternative) groups, which traffic in everything from techniques for anarchists and the best ways to (intentionally) destroy the earth to hard-core porn. See Figure 21.3 for a partial list of major alt. newsgroup topics. Access to the alt.* groups (found under the Other Popular Newsgroups icon) requires the full-access token. You'll find the e-form for requesting the token in the Internet Center folder. No matter how sophisticated you think you are, you'll find the range of topics in alt.erotica.* humbling.

Full-access privileges are by account, not by computer, so if you're the parent of a pre-adolescent or adolescent, you undoubtedly want to remove that token before giving your child his or her very own account—lest they become more precocious than you're comfortable with. And, of course, you should sit down and talk with your child about on-line do's and don't's, such as never giving your home address or phone number and reporting any uncomfortable on-line experiences to a parent.

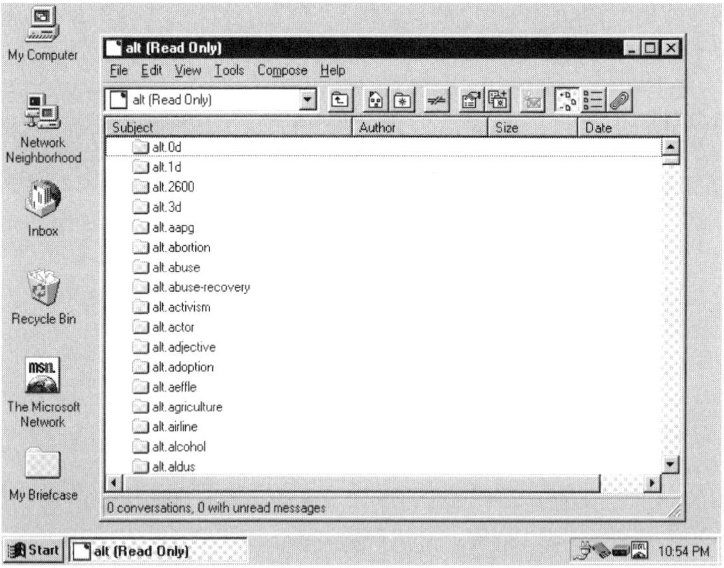

Figure 21.3 *The least controlled of all the Internet newsgroups, the alt. newsgroups, require a full access token and are accessible only to those over 18.*

Downloading Files

Much of the controversial stuff on the Internet is graphic (in several senses of the word) in nature. Unlike straight (no pun) text files, files found in the alt.binaries.* areas are, well, binary and need to be downloaded before you can offend yourself or others with them. Since the Internet doesn't support the direct transmission of full eight-bit binary files, you might think that the whole problem is rather self-limiting, but, once again, technology rides to the rescue. Most binary files on the Internet are posted in a format known as UUEncoded, which represents eight-bit binary files as longer seven-bit ASCII files. Many services that do allow posting impose limits on file size, sometimes as low as 50K. Thus, large files may be found posted in a seemingly ridiculous number of parts, generally indicated in the message header as part [Y/XXX]. (If this is geekspeak to you, don't worry; there's no pop quiz planned.)

A readily available (check the Internet Center File Library folder) freeware program called WinCode lets you encode and decode single and multipart UUE-formatted files quite simply. To download a binary file from the UseNet areas on MSN, you'll simply need to read the file by clicking on it in the normal manner, then save it using the Save As. command from the file menu. Once you've downloaded all the parts, start Wincode and use the File/Decode menu choice to open the first file. WinCode can work its way from part one of the chain through the remainder. Admittedly, this is not as clean as a regular MSN download, but you can use Windows 95's multithreading capability to download all the parts of a desired file simultaneously and browse other messages while the download progresses. Typical file formats for graphic files include .gif and .jpg for still images, .wav or .mdi for sound and music, and .avi (Windows video), .mpg, .mov, .gl, .dl, and .fli for multimedia/animated presentations. Viewers for all these file types are posted frequently in the various newsgroups that use these types and in the Internet Center File Library folder. And no, not all binaries are X-rated—you'll find lots of stuff from television and movie trailers in alt.multimedia, just a few keystrokes away from alt.multimedia.erotica. For an excellent and up-to-date overview of the newsgroups available, just click on the Roadmap to the Newsgroups icon in the Internet Newsgroups folder in the Internet Center.

In addition to the Internet Center, you'll find access to specific Internet newsgroups in the subfolders of many individual categories.

Web Browsing with the Internet Explorer

If you've installed the Internet Explorer option from Plus Pack, you'll also have an icon called World-Wide Web

(WWW) in your Internet Center folder as well as a separate Internet Explorer icon on your desktop. Clicking on either icon will launch the Microsoft Internet Explorer, a *web browser*, which is a graphical user interface for the Web, combining text, images, and hyperlinks (Figure 21.4). *Hyperlinks* are the key to understanding the Web—they let you flit from topic to topic and, more importantly, Web page to Web page all around the world. When you first start the Internet Explorer, it will open its default home page, which has the cumbersome address of http://www.home.msn.com. The bad news is that this is the short form of the full address (also known as a URL, for Universal Resource Locator). The good news is that you'll rarely, if ever, have to type cumbersome addresses such as this.

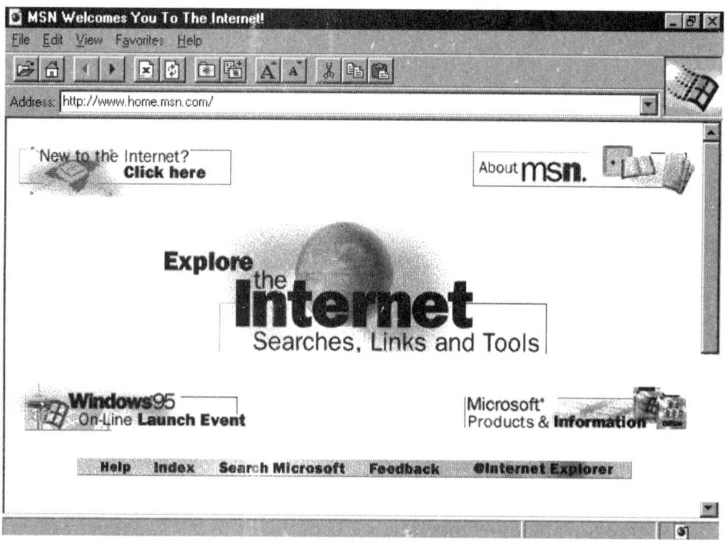

Figure 21.4 *The Microsoft web browser gives help in getting started and acts as a full interface to the WorldWideWeb.*

If you explore the MSN home web page with your mouse, you'll notice that clicking on any of the graphics or any of the underlined words will take you somewhere else, either within the page you're on or to an entirely new page. To go back to where you just were, click on the "back" button at the top of the page (it's next to the little button that looks like a house, which itself will bring you all the way back to the initial home page). Congratulations, you've just learned the hardest part of using the Web!

Other useful navigation concepts are:

1. The color of an underlined word changes after you've clicked on it. This color-coding allows you to see where you've already been if you are looking at a list of items that you might want to explore. You can customize the colors used for new or already visited shortcuts (another name for links) by selecting View|Options|Appearance.
2. You can save an address for easy access in a later session by going to the Favorites menu and selecting Add to Favorites, which creates a shortcut on the Favorites menu for later use.
3. The path of pages you've visited is automatically saved as shortcuts accessible via a list at the bottom of the File menu and also in the File menu item More History. By default, the Internet Explorer will keep track of the last 300 pages you've visited; you can increase or decrease the history tracking number by changing the value on the View|Options|Advanced tab page.
4. You're by no means limited to using the MSN home page as your starting page. You can make any page you like your default starting page by going to that page, opening the View|Options|Start Page tab page, and clicking on the Use Current (page) button. For example, one of the better-known on-line directories and search engines is called "Yahoo!" (Don't ask . . .). You can find it by clicking on the Explore the Internet graphic on the MSN home page and selecting Yahoo! from the

Explore the Internet page. Once you've gone to the Yahoo! home page (Figure 21.5), go to the View menu, select Options|Start Page, and click the Use Current button. If you later decide to go back to using the MSN home page as a default, reopen the Start Page tab and select Use Default.

Another thing you need to be aware of is that not all resources are on-line all the time (we're talking about interconnected computers all around the world here, so inevitably some percentage are being repaired or upgraded at any time) and that content may move from one host machine or address to another or be deleted by its owner. If you're trying to connect to a page you saw in the past and it seems that nothing has happened for a very long time, you can hit the stop button to abandon the link and explore

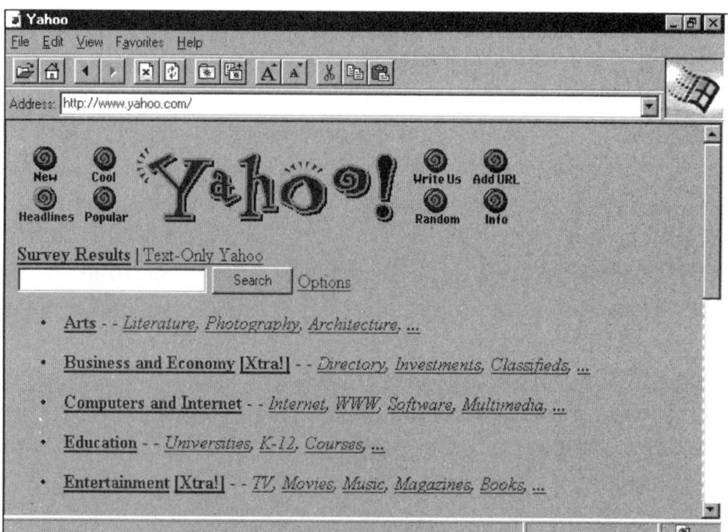

Figure 21.5 *Not limited to the Microsoft search engine, full advantage can be taken of others such as Yahoo!, one of the most popular on-line search engines.*

another. You can increase or decrease the text type size via buttons on the toolbar, and the usual copy, cut, and paste features are also available here.

To find material on a topic of interest, the search engines provided by free services like Yahoo and Lycos are invaluable. Just enter a few key words that describe what you're looking for, and hit the Search button. The trick is learning how much of a description to search for—too little (like searching for "the"), and you get everything on the net; too much, and you don't get to see pertinent topics that are phrased a bit differently.

Downloading Files with the Internet Explorer

Long-time Internet users are probably wondering what happened to those old standby tools *ftp* (standing for file transfer protocol) and *telnet* (a program that allows you to control a distant computer as if you were directly logged into it), which are conspicuously absent from MSN's Internet access features. This omission may be due to the limitations on speed and access for MSN in its early phases—telneting or ftping at even 28.8 kilobaud can be painfully slow. When MSN opens up for faster access via ISDN modems and/or direct network TCP/IP links, these are going to be far more critical. While ftp and telnet don't show up as menu items, you can access them using the URLs, and, for ftp, can receive files the same way you would from a BBS in the Internet Center—you read it , then save it. To show how this works, we can use a search engine (Yahoo! in this case) to search for the phrase "Microsoft ftp." (Microsoft runs an ftp site to provide tech support and to let users download new drivers or patch files.) You may get more than one search result, but if you click on the one called ftp.microsoft.com, you'll get to the page shown in Figure 21.6, which will allow you to read and save any of the files or drill down into the folders. Double-clicking on a file will trigger a download to the Internet Explorer—when it's done, use Save As from the file menu to make a local copy of the file.

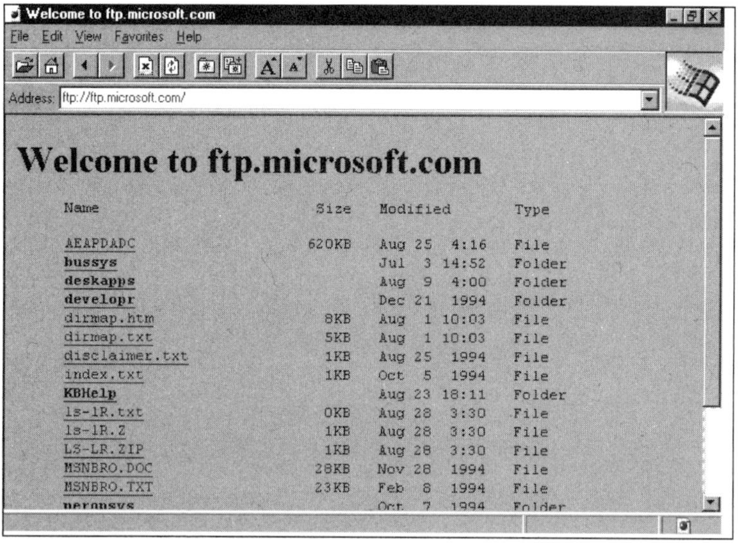

Figure 21.6 *The ftp is not directly available, but there are work-arounds.*

You can even telnet the same way—search for "telnet" and a target name in the search box, then click on the appropriate result. For example, if you've also got an account on CompuServe, you could log on to it via telnet (Figure 21.7), though logging on to CompuServe directly would be just as fast and cheaper, since you wouldn't be paying two networks for the privilege of connecting. There are many other sites you could ftp or telnet to around the world—if you can't find them on Yahoo! or Lycos or Microsoft Search, check out any of the Internet directories at your local bookstore for addresses, and modify the URL in the address field of the Internet Explorer as needed. Happy Web Surfing!

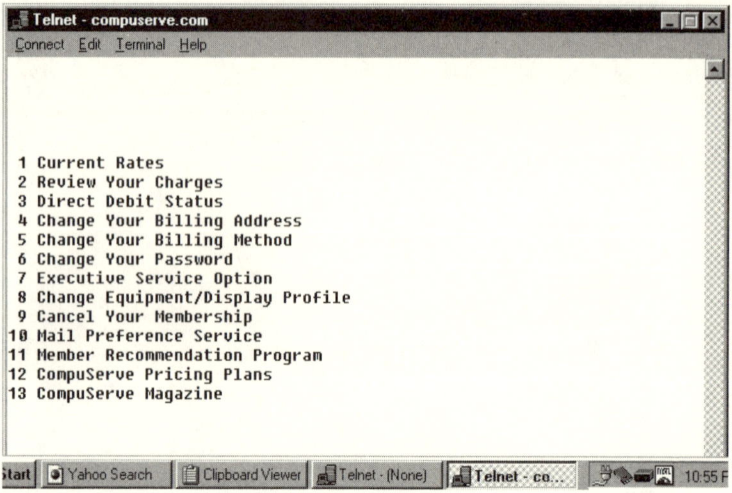

Figure 21.7 *A telnet session is launched from the Internet Explorer.*

APPENDIX

Bringing Your Business or Forum On-line

As you have probably gathered from this book, Microsoft is committed to making MSN the most compelling on-line service available. To that end they have not only designed a host of development tools but have made the process of bringing your business on-line relatively painless.

Becoming a Forum Manager

If business is not what you had in mind but you would like to have a special interest forum which is not currently available (these can include such topics as gardening, music, or any subject where you think others would enjoy participating and which is not currently available), these too are easy to set-up, or stage. Because of high volume, there are times that applications for forum management are not taken, but when they are, information is posted on how to submit an application in a category information folder. And, you can always E-Mail your thoughts and ideas to sysop@msn.com.

Becoming an Independent Content Provider

To become an Independent Content Provider you must provide Microsoft with a business plan. Necessary background information about your business including your name, address (postal and E-Mail), telephone and fax numbers, and your company's tax ID or license number is required. Also, how is your existing business structured? Is it a corporation, limited partnership, non-profit organization, sole proprietorship, or something else?

Of course, you also need to include a description of what you propose to do on-line! How will your business be interactive, and what, if any, will be your competition? What will make your business unique? Although your business is not required to be exclusive to MSN, you should tell Microsoft if you will be providing the same service on other on-line services.

Next, give some thought to how you would like to generate revenues on-line. As you have seen, this can take many different forms. There can be charges each time a file is downloaded, a monthly subscription charge, or even a one-time charge to enter an auditorium for a special event. These and others can be used alone or in combination.

Don't let the thought of a business plan intimidate you. Tools and guidelines are available to you right on MSN: From MSN Central, click on Member Assistance and then Maps and Information. From there click the ICP Information folder. You'll find Download and Run files summarizing the Microsoft Network and detailed descriptions on how to submit a business plan. After a period of time (it could even be a month or two, these folks are very busy) you will receive further information on how to proceed, including any new procedures and more detailed advice on any development tools which could be put at your disposal.

The more businesses participate, the more the on-line community will meet everyone's needs and the more enjoyable it will be for all. So join in, and everyone will benefit!

INDEX